THE SECRET TO HAPPINESS IS LOW EXPECTATIONS

THE SECRET TO HAPPINESS IS LOW EXPECTATIONS

Living with a Funny Bone,
a Wishbone, and a Backbone

ISABEL BOLT

Copyright © 2024
Isabel Bolt

Performance Publishing
McKinney, TX

All Worldwide Rights Reserved.

All rights reserved. No part of this publication may be reproduced, stored in a retrieval system or transmitted, in any form or by any means, electronic, mechanical, recorded, photocopied, or otherwise, without the prior written permission of the copyright owner, except by a reviewer who may quote brief passages in a review.

ISBN: 978-1-961781-59-7 (paperback)

PERFORMANCE
PUBLISHING

I dedicate this book to all of us who were born with a sense of humor and somehow manage to keep it.

Contents

Prologue	1
There's been a mistake. I got the wrong family.	5
The Labor Comes After the Delivery	13
The Lake House 1.0	25
If I can just make it through this week…	33
They shoot horses, don't they?	57
Let there be Light	71
Lake House 2.0	81
Starting Over. Late.	99
What's love got to do with it?	105
Extremely Loud, Incredibly Close	119
Rations & Rants	139
Flats are for Quitters	151
Starting over. Again.	159
Playing with Matches	171
The Corporate Package	183
I'm Suing Gabby for Secondhand Stress	197
Six Saturdays and a Sunday	207

*"There is no greater agony
than bearing an untold story inside you."*
– Maya Angelou

Prologue

Any way you look at it, life is full of *expectations*. Those you have for yourself. Those you have of others. Those others have of you. Mine have always been high. Across the board. It's an obsessive struggle. Incredibly, some people have very few *expectations,* or if they do, they keep them low. They seem happy to let things evolve. When you *expect* nothing, you are rarely disappointed. Perhaps, they are the smart ones.

After six decades, there's enough mileage in my rearview mirror for me to come to a few conclusions about *expectations*. Significant *expectations* that I desperately held on to – never happened. And I was heartbroken. Or strangely relieved. Other circumstances and events I never *expected* nor prepared for in a million years – happened. And I was shocked and terrified. Or filled with awe.

I *expected* to get where I pictured I was going. I am the quintessential destination person. Goals, lists, planning…a self-appointed Minister of Making Things Happen versus Letting

Things Happen. All the talk about "the journey"? That was something to be endured until I got to where I *expected* to arrive. And it would be extraordinary. And it has been. But not in the ways I *expected*.

~ ~ ~ ~ ~

Until recently, I never truly understood a poem I had to memorize in high school by Gwendolyn Brooks. *"Live not for battles won. Live not for the end of the song. Live in the along."* Slowly I am realizing that the quest to be successful and special is not reserved for the fleeting moment you reach the summit and plant your flag. It is actually the ordinary day-to-day comings and goings that shape us, guide us, and ultimately create the collage of our lives. The "along."

It's what made the *Seinfeld* sitcom a hit – according to producers, a show about "nothing". All the seemingly unimportant episodes and interactions in life that happen while we wait for those big plans and dreams to come to fruition – if, in fact, they ever do. Truth is, most don't – and if they do they are brief. True joy comes to us in everyday moments. Sometimes we miss it because we are preoccupied with capturing the "extraordinary". That goal in the distance…just around the next corner. If we pause long enough, we might notice that the seemingly ordinary episodes right in front of us are where the real treasure lives. Life's rhythm has a way of smoothing out all the wrinkles over time in ways you never *expected*.

THE SECRET TO HAPPINESS IS LOW EXPECTATIONS

As long as I can remember, I've kept a scrapbook. Comics, headlines, songs, sermons, funny things people said, touching moments that made my throat close, and hilarious episodes with family and friends. Later these were transferred from paper to a hard drive and the scrapbook grew, taking on a life of its own. It became my ad hoc journal. Whether I was the proverbial "windshield" or the "bug," the scrapbook continued behind closed doors.

For most of my life, success to me meant arranging people, places, and situations in a particular order and then keeping all of it together. Like a puzzle I could force to fit, then glue into place. Firmly. But more often than not, as much as I tried to wrestle it to the ground, my life took many turns I didn't *expect*. Moving to Texas, having children, working in the same industry for thirty years, buying a lake house, moonlighting as a writer, breast cancer, a divorce, post-marriage romance, my sister moving in, a recurrence of breast cancer, online dating. It's been a lesson in courage, grief, joy, vulnerability, faith, humility, saying "goodbye" and love. But mostly – *humor*.

On a subconscious level, this book was entirely *expected*. It is Gwendolyn's "along" and *Seinfeld's* homage to "nothing." A curated collection of the journey I was so anxious to fast forward. One filled with people, events, and circumstances that were quite *unexpected*. Despite my desperation to control every outcome, I can now see the true pearls were mostly *unexpected*, sometimes entertaining, often hilarious, occasionally profound, and all a part of a patchwork quilt not yet sewn together. Perhaps you will see yourself in some of my stories.

"There's been a mistake. I got the wrong family."
- Greg, six years old, after being put in a "time out"

"A dysfunctional family is any family with more than one person in it."
— Mary Karr

The scene of the crime was the Aragon Ballroom on Lawrence Avenue in Chicago, mid 1950s. That is where Rosella and Witold (my parents, Rose and Victor) met. My mother, thirty-four, and my father, forty. Both old enough to know better, but as Keith Morrison said on *Dateline* last week... *"In a way it was a dissertation on love. Love – intoxicating, impetuous, foolish. Love that lives like a fugitive in a long secret tunnel of regret."*

As the story goes, my mother rejected the suitor who wrote to her weekly during the war. He promised he would make her happy every day of her life. Begged on his knees to have my grandfather make her marry him. She wasn't feeling it. She left Chicago for California for a few "blissful" years (her words) but headed back to Chicago when she got worried my grandmother was getting too old to take care of herself. Gramma was forty-five at the time (and lived until ninety-two). She should have stayed in California.

A few years passed and my father – who was born in Poland, educated in Austria, and recently settled in Chicago – literally waltzed into her life. He said he was looking for someone beautiful who was Roman Catholic and could cook. Rosella was also born in Europe – Yugoslavia – an added bonus. My mother said she was looking for someone handsome and educated who would cherish her. They both got what they wanted except for the "cherish" part. I heard the story a thousand times about how the photographer had to tell Victor to kiss Rose on the church steps on their wedding day. At least the *expectations* were set low right from the beginning.

My father was happy with his newspapers, opera records, and stamp and coin collections. My mother wanted affection. She also wanted a family. They agreed on having a family.

Mom: *You think the Virgin Mary is something? It happened to me three times.*

Those immaculate conceptions turned into me, Andrew, and Joanna.

My mother was my first true love. She was loving, emotional, affectionate, and funny. But my father wore down her spirit. It was like watching a snowman slowly melt. She was desperately unhappy. I was desperate to make her happy. And that is how Codependents are born.

I loved my father too. He was not a bad man…just disconnected. From everyone except himself. He knew what he wanted 100% of the time and set about getting it.

Case in point: We never had a lot of money. Although my father was an engineer, he couldn't sign any drawings because he came from Poland which was communist after WWII, and we were in a Cold War. From what I was told, he designed some sort of product and in lieu of getting "credit" for it, his boss signed it as his own and gave my father a cash bonus as compensation.

Boss: *Buy your wife something for the house or take a nice trip together.*

My mother at the time had three children under five, two in diapers and no washing machine or dryer. My father took the money and flew to Paris. Alone. A different Cold War.

We lived in a "bungalow and a half" on the northwest side of Chicago called Jefferson Park. The "half" was an apartment upstairs my parents rented out for extra income. Downstairs, the five of us lived in a two-bedroom, one-bath house. Gramma and Grandpa lived in Logan Square. At the time, it looked more like stage set from *West Side Story* versus the vibrant neighborhood it is today with arts, music venues and trendy cocktail bars. My aunt – my mother's only sibling – and uncle and my four cousins escaped from the city to Elk Grove, a Chicago suburb. We got together often – holidays, anniversaries, graduations, birthdays, communions, confirmations – always celebrating something. At our house, the seven cousins would go down to the basement and prepare talent shows for after dinner. The adults were upstairs where lots of shouting, laughing, debating, and cooking was happening. The shouting was usually about baseball or politics. I couldn't wait until it was my aunt's turn to entertain. My cousins all had their own bedrooms on a second floor. In my twelve-year-old mind, this was how movie stars lived. Vacations were few and far between, but there were trips during the summers to Cedar Lake with Gramma's fried chicken and strudel and apple slices. Eventually Gramma and Grandpa sold their home and moved in upstairs from us, so we had the typical extended family, and it was good. Except for my father, who had just about enough of the one-sided exposure to my mother's side.

When I was fourteen, my father was hell bent on sending me to Poland – unchaperoned – to meet his sisters and their families. At the time Poland was behind the Iron Curtain. (*Let that sink in a minute. A child. Unchaperoned. Behind the Iron Curtain.*) When I got there, it was a surprise party. *He told them I spoke Polish and told me and my mother they spoke English.* Not even close. Six weeks of playing cards and charades. He was so pleased with himself that he got to show me off to his relatives; the end had justified the means. My grandmother didn't know who to kill first – her daughter or her son-in-law.

He was a dutiful father. Took us to piano lessons and church; read us classic fairy tales like *Hansel and Gretel*, *The Lion and the Mouse*, and *Pinocchio*; built us ice rinks and sandboxes in the backyard; took us on subway trips to museums in downtown Chicago. This is how he showed love. But it was arm's length. In retrospect, the enzyme or chromosome that forms emotional bonds and connections was missing.

Fast forward, I am dating Jeff, and he is at the dining room table with the extended family. We got into a lively discussion about something irrelevant and when the smoke cleared, we noticed Jeff's chair was empty. No one knew how long he was gone. Not in the bathroom. Not in the kitchen. I found him in the recliner in the basement. Said he couldn't take us shouting at each other. I explained, "It was a *conversation*." Good grief. I eventually understood his reaction when I had dinner at his house. Pretty quiet. A distinct lack of confrontation. How odd.

Months later, when I told my father that Jeff asked me to marry him, he looked over his newspaper and said, "*What is his degree in?*" That was the extent of his inquiry.

After our wedding, Jeff and I moved into married student housing at the University of Illinois, three hours south of Chicago. It had orange shag carpet, a mustard yellow refrigerator, and cinder block walls. In a year or so, Jeff graduated, earning two Master's degrees: one in Architecture and one in Business. Brilliant. Except it was the mid-1980's. The economy was in the tank. He was interviewing all over the U.S. We were probably not going back to Chicago. This was not what I *expected*. He hung a sign over our door: "*Tomorrow you can be anywhere.*" It sent me into convulsions. He got one job offer. One. In Dallas. All I knew about Dallas was the TV show with J.R. and Sue Ellen. We packed for Southfork.

Back to my "family of origin," as the therapists like to say...My mother sacrificed everything she could for the three of us. She adored us, but we could not fill the hole in the middle where my father should have been. Despite the condition of their relationship, she would not leave him, even years later after going back to work full-time when she could easily have supported herself. Her comment to me toward the end of her life: "*Thank God it never affected you children.*" Astonishing.

And so, between my mother confiding in me daily about her mistake in choosing a man who was never present for her, and my father's inability to truly feel another's joy or pain, or even feign interest...the *expectation* that I would be somebody's "little girl" never happened. That's a big disappointment. However.

You can't pick your parents. But Somebody does. And He doesn't make mistakes. My independence, sensitivity, confidence, and sense of humor are the direct result of inheriting this family. Who I am is either the collateral damage, positive effect, or both – depending how you want to look at it.

An entirely different chapter began when my folks decided to move and join us in Dallas in the late 1980s. Abandoning their home of thirty-three years in Chicago. In retrospect, this had everything to do with a full court press on my fertility – which was the furthest thing from my mind. The two people who raised me could not wait to get their hands on the next generation.

Only this time they were in perfect harmony.

The Labor Comes After the Delivery

"The days are long, but the years are short."
– Anonymous

I remember exactly when it happened. We were in Cancun on vacation. Things were going so well. We were settled in Dallas in our new home, our jobs seemed secure, a little money in the bank, feeling our groove, walking on the beach. Life was good.
Jeff: *I think it's time.*
Me: *For lunch?*
Jeff: *No. To start a family.*
We were married eight years by then. Of course, this conversation was inevitable.

People who know me will say I don't like children. That is not entirely true. At the time, I was ambivalent. Babies never interested me. When I was young, it was all about Barbie. She had Ken, a best friend Midge, and a sister named Skipper. Barbie was busy going to an important job in her convertible. No babies were in the picture. Growing up, I never babysat. On no occasion would you find me peeking in strollers clucking and cooing – unless it was filled with puppies. I didn't have that longing other women describe on how incomplete their lives would be without children.

Jeff definitely had the longing. But not even close to the enthusiasm my mother and father had about being grandparents. Andrew wasn't dating any one particular girl, and Joanna was in an apartment with four cats. My mom and dad had moved from Chicago to Dallas and bought a home four blocks away. And I assure you it wasn't to watch me driving a convertible to my big job.

> **Sidebar:** First, an introduction. Remember Ray's mother, Marie, from Everybody Loves Raymond? That's my mother. My father? A 75-year-old Sheldon from the Big Bang Theory. Only with a Polish accent.
>
> The week my parents moved into their new home, I brought a housewarming basket filled with Texas-related welcome gifts. There was a book on outlet shopping. My mother loved a bargain. It was a great book because it was sorted by category. So, if you were looking for the best deal on a washing machine, you could see all the places with the cheapest washing machines. Fantastic. (Take note – this was pre-Google.) Even better, I explained to my mother, on the front of each chapter was a map so you could plan your route and hit several places in a day.

Mom: *That's great honey. But how do they know where you are coming from?*
You can try, but there is no explaining that.

Not to be outdone, that same week, Jeff and I are over at their place, and my father is having trouble with the attic. Seems when you pull down the ladder, it doesn't reach the garage floor.
Jeff: *Vic, we'll have to pick up a ladder extension at Home Depot.*
My father just stared at him.
Vic: *No. I will be getting some cement. The garage floor has to be raised.*
My mother started laughing. Me too, then Jeff. The hysteria died down and we went home.
As we walked through the door the phone was ringing. It was my mother. Still laughing.
Mom: *Who ever heard of a ladder extension? Your father and I cannot get over that one.*
I had to send Jeff back over there before their whole kitchen was full of cement.
This is what we were dealing with.

~ ~ ~ ~ ~

Back to family planning. Jeff explained that since he had four sisters, and no brother, we must have a boy. And we would keep on going until we got one. He would love all the daughters that might come before…but a son would be part of the equation.

What I heard was: I better do everything in my power to make sure it was a boy right out of the gate.

And now I will tell you how we got David at Walgreens. If you care about tipping the scale to a boy or girl, listen carefully. It is not as random as you think. It's all about when you ovulate. The average cycle for a woman is 28 days. You ovulate somewhere in the middle, so let's call it 14. You ovulate on the 14th day. If your cycle is 32 days, it would be day 16, and so on. That's where I thought I was. And we would have had a houseful of Courtneys. I bought the magic ovulation kit and tested myself and it was actually day 19. Day 19 would be a boy because the boy sperms swim fast and die young. The girl sperms swim slow and are resilient, so any time before or after day 19 would be most likely a girl. Now we knew my day. Next I wanted to control the time of year I would have a baby.

I told Jeff, I didn't want to be nine months pregnant in Texas in September. Summer is too hot. Thanksgiving or Christmas were blacked out because I already have enough to do then. Stay away from July 1. That is my birthday. Our anniversary is early January, so let's keep that separate from birthday parties. Jeff tells people he had the NASA launch window.

Incredibly, David was conceived on the first try and was born in mid-April. The eagle had landed.
For me, pregnancy and delivery were like falling off a log. It was the taking-the-baby-home part that wasn't natural. He was

so perfect. I couldn't believe they let us just walk out of the hospital with him.

Like every new mother on the planet, I fell in love. It's different when it's yours. My milk came in, in buckets. Nursing was my favorite part even though that meant being up every couple hours around the clock. In between, I would wake up and check on him to be sure he was breathing. I was getting no sleep. Luckily, my office manager at the time did some witchcraft with maternity leave and vacation and personal days and I got close to six months off. Because I wouldn't be totally "vested" at work for three more months after that, my mother and father agreed they would watch David November through February. This was a godsend for all of us.

My mother was in heaven. My father was building a sandbox next to his tomato plants.
I, on the other hand, was a zombie. Mostly because David still wasn't sleeping through the night – and wouldn't until eleven months. My mother's diagnosis? I had *"nervous milk"*. And as delighted as she was to be with David, there were endless guilt trips on how anyone could leave a baby for six to eight hours a day to work. My grandmother also chimed in…*"You are nothing like your cousin. She really wanted her baby."* Good grief.

February came, I got my "vesting," and I quit The Corporation. I wondered. Maybe I was one of those career girls who was a "closet" stay-at-home mom. Maybe I never realized this was my true calling. My grandmother was fully supportive.

Gramma: *This is good — you should be home for Jeff.*
Me: *Jeff's at work.*
Gramma: *You should be there in case he calls.*

On David's nine-month birthday, three months ahead of the schedule posted in the baby reference bible, he stood up and walked across the room. Now it was a different ball game. By his first birthday, he was finally sleeping through the night, which gave him even more energy. Constant motion and curiosity.

Jeff went to Home Depot to get the childproof locks. He spent an entire Sunday battening down the hatches. The kitchen, the bathrooms, our bedroom…it was a contraption you had to push, turn, and squeeze to release. Jeff walked into the kitchen from the garage after storing the drill to see David toddling over to the cabinet under the sink. Push-turn-squeeze-release, the child cracked the safe. Back to Home Depot Jeff went and started all over with the industrial strength locks. Going forward it would take me twenty minutes to make dinner and forty minutes to open cabinets.

The first few months staying home were a novelty. I had worked since I was fourteen. Now, there was no boss to report to. Except the one in the crib.

By any measure, David was precious. Happy, loving, smart. The problem was between the feeding and changing and dressing and cleaning up, I was in my robe until noon. My mother was there at a moment's notice if I needed to be somewhere, but there weren't many places I needed to be anymore.

Meanwhile, my husband and mother were conspiring to hypnotize me into believing that having an only child was tantamount to child abuse. It was late summer, and David was splashing around in the baby pool in our backyard. Playing with buckets and cups.
Jeff: *Look how lonely and miserable he is.*
Me: *Go get your swim trunks on and play with him.*
Jeff: *You know what I mean. He needs a brother.*
Me: *Oh, for god's sake.*

I figured I better comply before I lost my nerve. I didn't want kids five years apart. I drove to Walgreens. Another NASA launch. The second time we tried, Gregory arrived. Late July. Jeff was getting good at this.

We came home with the baby and put him in David's lap.
David: *I promise I won't take his head off, Daddy.*
Jeff: *That's a good start, son.*

Back to a familiar routine of being up round the clock. I desperately missed the sleep, but nursing was still my favorite part. David had been all business – ten minutes on each breast and he was done. Greg liked to nuzzle and cuddle and doze in between breasts. So, every two hours became a blur because he didn't want to leave my arms. I don't think I ever got out of my robe.

Around week three:
David: *Mommy, I don't think Greg's mommy is coming to get him.*
Me: *What should we do?*
David: *Can we keep him, and you be his mommy?*
The pure sweetness of that request still makes me tear up.

But then there was the matter of the day-to-day. The time I discovered Greg had chicken pox the day of his Christening. Threw a blanket over him and the show went on. Going to Kohls with the boys to get David new shoes, and he was so excited that by the time we tried on a dozen pairs, we lost the pair he walked in with. I just left them there. The shoes, not the boys. Greg had a cloth diaper he liked to carry with him like Linus in the *Peanuts* cartoon. When it was worn down to a rag, I replaced it with another diaper, but it didn't have the blue stitching on it. He wouldn't accept a substitute. Locating blue-stitched diapers was the equivalent of finding the Holy Grail. This was pre-Amazon. It took a week and fifteen stores by the time I finally found the brand with the stitching.

Then there was the afternoon I was feeding David in the highchair. The Cowboys were beating the Lions in the playoffs. Then the Lions kicked the winning field goal.
Me: *Fuck*
David: *Fuck, fuck, fuck.*
In walked my parents: *What is he saying?*
Me: *Yes.* FORK, *spoon, knife. We are learning utensils.*

THE SECRET TO HAPPINESS IS LOW EXPECTATIONS

Stood in line for two hours to see Dallas' legendary "real" Santa Claus at NorthPark mall. When it was finally our turn, Greg was crying inconsolably. So was I. I lived for "Mother's Day Out" at the church where I could sneak the kids in and out without my own mother knowing so I could have a few hours to myself.

I was beyond fortunate to have my mother close by, but her "help" spilled over into other areas.
"How do you work in this left-handed kitchen?"
Home from the salon. *"Don't worry, your sister's hair didn't turn out either."*
"Do you like your sofas facing that way?"
And the final straw – me picking up David at my parent's house after being at an appointment. He toddles over.
"Oh, he'll go to anybody."

David turned three; Greg was one. I had settled into a routine but unsettled inside. I didn't feel like any of the mothers you see or hear about who are self-actualized through their children. The ones pictured in white flowing gowns holding hands through wildflowers. At the playground waiting breathlessly at the bottom of a slide. Pushing a stroller through Disney World. God, no. Compound that with my mother.
"Aren't two healthy beautiful boys enough for you?"
It was a fair question.

In the afternoons, if and when the boys took naps, I would watch soap operas. *Days of our Lives, All My Children, The Young and the Restless.* One day, I was feeling particularly vulnerable and one of the story lines took its toll. I started crying and I couldn't stop. I do not cry pretty. In fact, everything gets red and swollen – eyes, nose, lips. I actually won an ugly crying contest at the lake house girl's slumber party after watching John Travolta in that movie where he has a brain tumor. Heartbreaking.

Back to the situation.
Jeff, coming home from work, walks in from the garage to the kitchen. I am at the sink. He stops.
Jeff: *What happened to you?*
Me: (crying) *Meredith broke up with Jason for Josh who was waiting for a heart transplant and then Jason got killed in a car wreck and he donated his organs and guess who got his heart? Josh.*
Jeff: *Oh my God. Is this someone from church?*
Me: *No. It's* All My Children.
Jeff: *Okay. I think you might need to see Dr. Gloss about some hormones or something.*
I made the appointment with the OB/GYN whom I had been seeing for ten years. She delivered both boys. Knew me well. I told her I think I have AIDS or something. Everything hurts, I'm depressed, tired all the time…
Doctor: *Isabel, are you having unprotected sex with strangers?*
Me: *Of course not.*
Doctor: *Are you an IV drug user?*
Me: *No.*
Doctor: *I have a prescription for you.*
She hands me a piece of paper. On it, it says, "GO BACK TO WORK".

And I did. My former employer had no openings at the time, but Gabby (my best friend from The Corporation) told me one of the other leaders in the industry we worked in was hiring. I got an interview. I was hired. Although logistics took a while to nail down, I felt a strange relief. I was back in my high heels with a schedule. The boys were enrolled in pre-school around the corner. This felt like the answer.

That first week I picked them up after work. The principal was waiting for me at the front desk. He hands me a brown paper bag. Full of condoms. Apparently David raided our bathroom drawer, put them in his overalls and distributed them to his classmates.
Principal: *You might want to consider locks for your cabinets.*

~ ~ ~ ~ ~

A very important question was answered in those two years. When I quit The Corporation, I wondered. *"Could I be a stay-at-home mom? Maybe children were my true calling?"*
A categorical "No."

A failure? Absolutely not. Being a mother brings out a softness, a fierceness, awe, and pride – at a depth and in a gear you didn't know you had. No job or achievement, however grand, can simulate the experience. I knew for sure; I was not cut out to be a stay-at-home mom. But I was a grateful, devoted mom, nonetheless. If you are a mother, however flawed, and whatever your choices, you understand.

The Lake House 1.0

"It was the best of times. It was the worst of times."
– Charles Dickens

"When you go through Deep Water, I will be with you…"
– Isaiah 43:2

Lake houses are very similar to other undertakings that spark romantic illusions where the *idea* of something has little to do with the *reality* of that something. It is right up there with getting a puppy, backpacking through Europe, and quitting your day job to stay home with the children. I've done all of it. So, I can tell you from experience that, while similar, over time, the lake house established a category all its own.

It all started innocently enough in the early years of our marriage when Jeff and I were invited to a distant relative's lake house for fourth of July. We were sitting on the steps.

Jeff: *We should get a lake house*

Me: *Why?*
Jeff: *So, we can spend time with the kids on the weekends at a lake.*
Me: *We don't have any kids.*
Jeff: *But when we do…*

Let me explain that Jeff never daydreamed. Not before every fact was on an Excel spreadsheet and each hypothesis was examined so thoroughly that the possibility that was even remotely considered ceased to exist. Which is why I chalked it up to heatstroke.

Fast forward ten years.
Jeff: *We should get a lake house.*

Oh no. This again. What was the matter with him?

Our situation was this: We were living in a starter home in an area where real estate was trending in the wrong direction; so, looking for a real house was a priority. I had just gone back to work – doctor's orders – after being home with the kids for two years. (See "The Labor Comes after Delivery.") Jeff was new in his job. We both traveled in our positions. His parents had recently joined mine in moving from Chicago to Texas, so things were getting complicated. And we had no disposable income.

So, we bought a lake house at Cedar Creek Lake, ninety minutes southeast of Dallas. It was 1994. The kids were two and four. It was a cute A-frame at the end of a channel with no water in front. Turns out we got a great deal on it. In a few months the water filled back up to knee-high. I got a big commission check and Jeff got a promotion; so somehow the mortgages were getting paid. We moved in some used furniture and started painting. It became the weekend destination for all our family and friends.

Soon we got a good deal on a used boat. These "good deals" are not hard to find after a dry spring when there is no water in the lake. That first summer, we "visited" our boat in dry dock. Early fall, after a wet September, we were able to move it six doors down from our house. We rented a slip from a neighbor who had waist-high water at the time. What a celebration that was. But you know what they say:
What is <u>the second best</u> day of your life?
Answer: Buying a boat
What is the <u>best</u> day of your life?
Answer: Selling it
What do "they" know, anyway?
Answer: Plenty
As we were about to find out over the next sixteen years.

There were kid parties, family get-togethers, girlfriend sleepovers, and a regional meeting for my office. And it was all good. Mostly.
Except for...

The Friday we arrived after work to find fifteen head of cattle in our backyard. They had knocked down our "rancher" neighbor's fence. The children were enchanted sitting on the deck seeing cows so close up. Cows are a bit bigger when they are on your lawn. And so are the cow pies we scooped up all weekend.

The nights when either Gabby's kids or mine were sick and we met in the kitchen at two a.m. with bleary red eyes trying to find the cough medicine, allergy medicine, or children's Tylenol. It was never far from the Advil we were taking.

The month when both the A/C and the refrigerator broke. We were able to pay off both with the money we were going to use for our vacation.
My mother: *Who needs a vacation? You have a lake house.*
I didn't know where to start, so I let that go.

Sometimes there is comfort in knowing what you will never do again, like having a regional planning meeting in a 1000-square-foot "cabin". I honestly don't know what I was thinking inviting sixteen of my co-workers down to the lake. Just anticipating the whole day gave me an upset stomach and sore throat which became a handy excuse when I literally exited stage right and handed Gabby the keys. Yes, I left my own party after the grill toppled over and burned the deck, people MIA because they couldn't find the house, and then, both toilets went out. Wouldn't flush. I was mortified. Called in sick to the event I was hosting. Got in the car and drove back to Dallas. Sorry. Not sorry. Found out later, *everyone stayed.* Had a blast. Cannot figure that out. Talked and laughed about it for years. A fond memory for all but me.

THE SECRET TO HAPPINESS IS LOW EXPECTATIONS

One of the most requested stories on the hit parade was what happened at the get-together I had with six of my best friends from work. We called ourselves the Steel Magnolias. One weekend we had a pajama party punctuated by a Sunday brunch boat ride around the lake.

It was my first time on the boat without Jeff. Of course, weeks prior, he insisted on boating lessons before he would let me take the boat out.

This was worth at least three semester hours.

Getting the boat in and out of the slip, what all the instruments did, emergency flares and fire extinguishers, safety, storage, life vests, lights, how to wrap and secure it when we were done…on and on. But what Jeff stressed the most – at least one semester hour – was the water level. I had to understand I would break the motor if I didn't pull it up way before the slip because it was so shallow by the dock. We had a dry run, (no pun intended.) I passed. The day arrived.

And here is where things went off the rails.

There were seven of us and three coolers. One water and mixers, one wine and vodka, the other full of snacks. It was tight. Maybe if we got rid of the extra gas tank, we would be more comfortable. Gabby, who had several boats in her younger days tested the gas tank and proclaimed it "topped off." I wasn't sure, but she said it like five times, so that made it true. Off we went. Abandoning the red tank on the dock.

I felt so empowered. Slowly cruising by all the pretty houses, then stopping to anchor so everyone could swim. An idyllic quiet Sunday morning. We started up across the other side of the lake, another round of mimosas and vodka cranberries. Of course, I wasn't drinking since I was the captain, but it was so good to see everyone else relaxing and…hang on, something felt off. We were drifting. I didn't hear anything. Like an engine. Oh no. The key was turning but nothing was happening. Dead silence in the back from Mrs. "Topped Off."

We were out of gas in the middle of the lake. No one around. It was eerie. Claire said we would be fine because there was plenty to drink. The other girls agreed there was nothing to worry about. Mostly because they were all under the influence. On the other hand, I had total grasp of the situation. It's tough to be the only sober one when things go south.

We waited. And then we saw them. Two men in a bass boat about a mile away. They looked like a couple dots on the horizon. We started yelling. Nothing. Then Sylvie took off her life vest and started waving her arms. I'll stop here to explain Sylvie is a 38 triple E so there was some bouncing involved and that bass boat hurled toward us at lightning speed. (Reminds me, I never properly thanked her.) Back to the men. They were delighted to rescue us and give us a tow back to our dock. They tied our boat to theirs and we started toward our channel. The girls continued toasting. I couldn't breathe. It felt like we were bobbing in a giant bath toy. I was terrified about the shallow water and keeping the engine up. We were getting close. I had the men stop twenty yards before the dock.

Men: *Is it the slip with the gas can on it?*

Me: *Yes.* (very funny)
Men: *How deep is it here?*
Me: *About three feet.*
Men: *We'll have to pull you in.*
One of them jumped in, holding the rope. We all went to the side of the boat when he disappeared. Only his hat and his cigarettes floated to the top. He bobs up.
A Furious Man: *THREE FEET??*
Me: *OH, NO! SORRY, SORRY, SORRY. My husband said it was shallow.*
Cory: (West Texas drawl) *Oh, and he got his haaat weeht.*
The men got us in. They left. The girls toddled out of the boat. Angie stayed back to help me cover and secure the boat until I realize we just wrapped the keys inside, so we did it all over again. I cannot remember ever being so tired.

Don't think for a minute it was all hard labor. For everyone else, it was Disneyland. The fishing, swimming, frog catching, marshmallow burning. All the summer holidays and cookouts. Friends, Gramma and Coppa, Nani and Papa, Aunty Joanna and Uncle Andrew. The lake house was THE destination for fun. Maybe the biggest labor of love was the tree house Jeff built with and for the boys. As an architect, this would be no ordinary tree house. It was spectacular. We probably should have added it to the square footage of the house when we eventually traded up.

When we bought the house, Jeff said, *"This will never make us a lot of money, but it will always be an investment in memory futures."* And he was never so right. We were five years in, and the memories were just beginning.

With one noteworthy detour.

But first... ⋀

If I can just make it through this week...

"*Living with kids and dogs is like running a blender without the top.*"
– Jerry Seinfeld

David (seven years old): *Daddy, I would really like a sister.*
Jeff: *Well, then we'd have to get a new mommy.*

People write books about raising children. Some people even read them. I find this comical. It would be like reading a book about swimming and then jumping off the high dive into ten-foot waves. Study all you want, but nothing can prepare you. This is a particularly hard realization for a woman like me who successfully planned conception and delivery down to the day…and when the children arrived, all hell broke loose. And it was way more entertaining than I *expected*. Note I did not say "fun." Fun for me is complete control, which is an illusion shattered into pieces when you have children.

Once David was certain we were keeping Greg, he became his full-time shepherd. I was nursing Greg and talking softly to him.
David: *You know he can't talk back yet, right, Mommy?*

It actually took Greg a while to communicate, probably because David never stopped talking. And hasn't stopped to this day. Joanna was babysitting once and swears Greg was speaking Korean, asking for something. David stepped in. *"He wants you to go in his toybox and get the red construction truck."*

Although he appreciated his big brother playing interpreter, Greg was less amused when David began to dress him in costumes. Cowboys, superheroes, Disney characters, ball players. I would go to Dillard's to buy tights in different colors. *"How old is your daughter?"* the woman in the kid's department would ask. I would say, *"Four."* No need to go into details. There were an endless stream of characters.

Me: *David, pick up your clothes.*
David: *Mommy, say "Cowboy, pick up your clothes."*
The next day.
Me: *Cowboy, can you put those toys away before Gramma and Coppa get here?*
David: (exasperated) *I'm not a Cowboy or Ratigan. I'm Joshua Hernandez, acting like Ratigan.*
As if to say, *"Keep up."*

THE SECRET TO HAPPINESS IS LOW EXPECTATIONS

And at the haircut place. Miss Angel was our barber. David is dressed as Captain Planet.
Miss Angel: *I see you are Captain Planet. Can you fly?*
David: (Looks at me then at her.) NO, I just PRETEND.
How can you keep a straight face?

While David was in fantasyland, Greg's curiosity was always more literal.
Case in point: Jeff steps out of the shower. Greg, two years old, toddles over and puts his finger on Jeff's penis. "*Eeuwh. Yuck*"
Jeff: *That's what your mother says.*
Which is not true.

They were both fascinated with anatomy, marriage, and babies. I'm in my bathing suit.
David: *Mommy, are those your breasts?*
Me: *Yes.*
David: *Do you drink milk out of them every day?*
Me: *No, you and Greg did when you were babies but now there are no babies in the house so no more milk.*
David: *Were me and Greg in your tummy when we were babies?*
Me: *Yes*
David: *Did you swallow us?*

At IHOP for Mother's Day when the boys are four and six.
David: *Daddy, how do newborn babies get into a mommy's tummy?*
Jeff starts explaining spermatozoa and the vas deferens.
David: *You are kidding.*
That stopped them cold for several years.

Meantime, Greg comes home to announce he is marrying his preschool teacher, Miss Pam.
"But don't be sad, Mommy. I will marry you, too, but that one will be in a church."
Glad he got that straight.

David, however, wants to marry classmate Megan. And when a baby comes out of her tummy it will be a boy and they will name him Peter. Then he will have a brother for Peter and name him Pan. I am instructed to buy a wedding cake for his school birthday party because Megan will be there. But it should say *Happy Birthday* in case she says, "*No.*"

Greg, five, is at Kroger with me. We are standing in a long line with our groceries.
Greg in a loud voice: *When are you and daddy going to get married?*
People turn to look at me.
Me: *We've been married sixteen years.*
Greg: *I didn't see it.*
When we got home, I had to go into the attic to find our wedding album as proof.

It was always astonishing to see how two boys who came out of the same womb, raised in the same house could look at life so differently. And they never changed. To this day. David – joyful, sensitive, serene, dreaming. Greg – also sensitive, but with a heavy dose of logic, common sense, and anxiety as to how everything fits together. David's mantra, *"Just think about all the possibilities."* Greg is more like, *"When I figure this out, I will own it."*

THE SECRET TO HAPPINESS IS LOW EXPECTATIONS

A perfect example was the morning I was rushing to get to the airport for a sales presentation in Arkansas. David took the bus, as usual, but Greg had a costume to bring to his sixth grade history class. Which I found out about at eight p.m. the previous evening. He was supposed to be Alexander Hamilton. "*Don't worry,*" he said. "*We can make the ruffled shirt out of coffee filters...*" Brilliant.

But I only mention that to say we were in the car with the costume. My mind was already on the PowerPoint slides I would be giving over lunch when a random question comes out of the backseat.
Greg: *Mom, can a virgin have a baby?* (What class did this come out of?)
Me: *No.*
Me: *Wait... Yes. Technically a man's sperm is put in a tube. Then the doctor puts it in a lady, and she can have a baby.*
Long pause.
Greg: *Mom?*
Me: *Yes?*
Greg: *Thanks for doing it the hard way.*

I did plenty of things the hard way. One of them was being born a female, identifying as one and acting like one. I understand this will completely unhinge many people. And it gets worse. We encouraged the boys to play with trucks and guns and action figures. Jeff would work in the yard and fix things around the house. I would grocery shop, cook, and do laundry. We didn't intentionally set out to raise two alpha males. But I'm really proud we did. They are an endangered species.

Jeff was driving David, seven, to peewee football. They are barely out of our subdivision when David yells, *Stop!*
Jeff: *What?*
David: *Look. Over there.*
Jeff: *I don't see anything.*
David: *Right over there.*
He points.
Jeff: *What are you pointing at?*
David: *There's a WOMAN mowing the lawn.*
He could not get over it.

Around the same time, Jeff is doing landscaping and David is "helping" him. The HVAC guy we were expecting pulls up, says hello, and goes toward the front door.
David to Jeff: *You going to keep planting bushes?*
Jeff: *Yes, why?*
David: *Then I'll go in and protect mom.*

This view of gender distinction I encouraged backfired a bit one day when I flew in from a work trip (obediently spreading the gospel according to The Corporation) and picked the boys up in after-school care. They were six and eight.
Me: *Boys, we have a nice three-day weekend ahead. It's Labor Day.*
David: *What's Labor Day?*
Me: *Well, it's a national holiday where the United States honors everyone who works to make this a great country. So, all workers get the day off.*
David: *Greg, when we get home, let's remember to thank Dad.*

David was not alone. Occasionally Greg would pipe up along similar lines.

Me: *Greg, you have to be really quiet. Mommy has to make an important call to her boss.*

(phone rings and goes to voicemail)

Me: (to myself) *Damn. I have to try later.*

Greg: *What's the matter? Wasn't daddy there?*

Hmmm.

Things were getting way too predictable, so when the boys were nine and eleven we adopted a new member of the family…an English Pointer. His name was Tanner, and we got him from a rescue shelter. Later it was clear who needed a rescue. He was a sixty-five-pound toddler with an anxiety disorder. A bird dog, Tanner was so hyper, his freckles vibrated even when he was still. Tanner and I shared the same personality – he just had two extra legs. At the time, we still had my eighteen-year-old cat who threw up everything she ate and was incontinent. I had to feed her baby food for low red blood count. Then Greg got a guinea pig. Named her Angel Dove Grace. No one knows where that came from. The name. Not the pig. She swoons on his chest as he plays the harmonica. Which is a welcome sound when compared with David practicing the trumpet. So, if you are counting, we had two houses, two kids, three animals, a trumpet, and a harmonica.

To stem the anxiety, I started going to Yoga twice a week. I would leave class, so calm and centered. It usually lasted right up until I pulled into the garage. Where I would learn things like Angel Dove Grace had eaten all the buttons off the TV remote.

Now David is thirteen. He loves all sports, but particularly football. He was and is a true "student of the game." Could hold his own against grown men when it came to strategy, stats, and technique. During the middle school playoffs, we watched from the stands as David walked over to his coach and said something. After the game we asked what he told the coach. *"I didn't tell him anything. I asked if he was open to some suggestions."*

When Greg was eleven, he accompanied Jeff to Karate lessons. It was good father/son time together. Greg used this opportunity to consult with his dad on questions like, *"Why don't good and food rhyme?"* and *"Do crocodiles have a penis?"* and *"How do you hotwire a car?"* Greg loves construction and figuring out how things work. He claims he got his father's "building birth defect."

Around that time, Greg set out to get a girlfriend.
He told me his strategy: *You go up to someone you like and say, "I like you and will you go out with me?" Sometimes they say, "Yes," and sometimes "No."*
Me: *Well, don't your feelings get hurt when they say "no?"*
Greg: *Oh, no, Mom…there are so many of them.*
Greg will be in sales.

Inspired by a 2003 article in the *Wall Street Journal* on the economic value of a college education, Jeff created an Excel matrix for the boys to show them the value of getting a good education, a good job, and the impact of a lifetime of saving and investing.

Jeff (in his best Ward Cleaver voice): *If you go to college and save $100 per month starting when you are twenty-two...*

David was missing something on ESPN, so he patted his father's head and left.

Greg, though, was intrigued. Jeff was playing that Excel spread sheet like a Stradivarius.

Greg (looking at the bottom line): *You mean if I get a college degree and start saving money at twenty-two that by the time I am forty I can be a millionaire?*

Jeff: *That is exactly right. This is what I am trying to teach you.*

Greg: *But I have one question.*

Jeff: *What?*

Greg: *Why didn't you do this for yourself?*

Ahem.

And if you think Jeff was failing in his attempt to counsel the boys on finances, he was doing even worse in their interpretation of his career. Speaking of careers, by now, I had switched back to The Original Corporation courtesy, yet again, through Gabby being my career version of a bird dog and my yearning to return to the Steel Magnolias. The job that was open at the time was straight commission. Make no mistake – contract furniture was never what I deliberately chose as a career, but it was a solid place to land until I was discovered. I would be an awesome white Oprah. Any day now.

Back to Jeff. We had always done a spring break ski trip. Now it was in jeopardy.

Me: *David, spring break is coming soon, and I want to talk to you about it. We are not going to be able to do as much as usual because we don't have a lot of extra money.*

David: *Why not?*

Me: *Well, Mommy only makes money when she sells something, and no one is buying anything.*

David: *Why don't you get a different job?*

Me: *What kind would that be?*

David: *The kind like Dad has, where they pay you just for showing up.*

Ouch.

While we were obvious failures to our children in the finance and career department, we were committed to bringing them up in the church. At David's birth, Jeff and I decided to ditch the idea of being next-gen Catholics. We didn't believe in the stain on the newborn's soul, and the priest talking to God on our behalf, among other things, so we became Methodists.

Sidebar: Jeff and I decided to take a Disciple course at our church where you study the Bible for a year. Since we were raised Catholic and let the priest do it for us, we thought we might read it ourselves now that we are Methodists. It was a great thing to do as a couple.

The discussions in our small group were always interesting. Like when we were in the Old Testament reading about the Tower of Babel and how God came down to punish

> the arrogance of those who lost sight of who they were building the tower for. He made it so none of them spoke the same language and caused utter confusion. *Jeff wanted to know, when did God come down and fix it so men and women couldn't understand each other?* No one had an answer.
>
> Our children exhibited a strong spiritual curiosity. Greg wanted to know one Sunday, *"What was Jesus' last name?"* And David was astonished when he found out that the church didn't adopt "The Hail Mary" from the NFL…it is really the other way around. I'm not sure the message was getting through, but we went most Sundays anyway.

There is a country song that goes, *"I know what I was feelin', but what was I thinkin'?"*

When Greg was twelve, we got a Lab puppy. Eight weeks old with feet the size of baseball gloves. His father was 125 pounds. At seven months he was seventy pounds. We got him for Greg since Tanner was David's dog. We named him Champ but all he ever heard was "No" and "No bite", so he thought that was his name. We had his AKC papers that confirmed he was a Labrador. But I think he was part Lab – part alligator. A Labigator.

Tanner seemed to have calmed down. But it is probably like forgetting your bum knee when you are hit with a migraine. There is a T-shirt that says, *"If you can't be a good example, be a terrible warning."* Here is my warning: *If you have walls, rugs, furniture,*

or shoes in your house, settle for a miniature poodle. When we left the house we put Champ behind a gate. When we returned, Tanner was behind the gate and Champ was in the den. Tanner is a mixed breed, but no dummy.
Greg: *How much did Champ cost?*
Me: *When we bought him, or since we've had him?*
Champ was perfectly trained. He pooped under the piano twice a day. Tanner was perfectly trained too. He knocked the front door down every time he heard the doorbell on the Domino's commercial.

We still had Angel, the guinea pig who was supposed to live two years and was now seven. Greg pulled a fast one by coaxing us into joint custody of a leopard gecko named Tango. We are sharing Tango with the Hathaway family. Did you know you have to feed geckos live crickets? Did you also know they live an average of twenty-five years? So, for a while it looked like Jeff and I would retire with a guinea pig and a gecko unless we could sell the house and leave before the Hathaway's notice. At night at our house you could hear squeaks, chirps, screams, and barks. The screams would be me.

The good news was both boys were doing great in school. This couldn't have happened at a better time, since we could no longer understand their homework. Turns out I was also geographically challenged.

I made the boys lunch almost every day. One day, Greg (uncharacteristically) forgot his lunch. So, I jumped in the car on the way to work and headed to the middle school. Went into the Principal's office.

Me: *Can you have someone deliver this lunch to Greg's class?*

Woman behind desk: *Ma'am, Gregory has not been in this school for two years.*

There were three stay-at-home-bulletin-board-mothers stapling hearts to the Valentine's Day board. Their staplers paused in mid-air. They looked me up and down in my heels and suit, as if to say…well, you know what they wanted to say.

Me: (small voice) *Where is he?*

Woman: *Intermediate school.*

Me: *Oh.*

I had enough sense not to ask where that was. I waited until I was outside and asked the maintenance man.

There are always lots of boys in and out of the house. One morning I went down in my nightgown and met Cole coming up the stairs looking for a T-shirt. Got my coffee and met Luke coming down the stairs with socks. Neither Greg nor David were home. Turns out they were at someone else's house. All the mothers get together once a year to sort laundry.

My favorite years of all were the teen years.

David was and is a football fanatic, which is a religion in Texas. He was starting middle linebacker for JV and two weeks into the season was drafted to the varsity roster. He eventually became one of the team captains in senior year. Because he was "double dipping," he was up at six a.m. for JV practice, home at six p.m.

from varsity practice, ran out three nights a week and Saturdays to coach a peewee team, and watched ESPN in between.

I have to stop here and set the stage for the spectacle that was *Friday Night Lights* in our suburb. Our little community had about 25,000 people and one high school. The football team had a 63-1 record over four years at the time. We were three-time State Champs of Texas in 5A Division II and the mythical national champs on the high school level. This was a big deal.

At the Athletic Booster Fund Raising Auction, dinner with the coach went for $3500. A helmet signed by all the players went for $5000. Tickets sell out in hours. The games are televised by FoxSports. Keith and Amy have access to their neighbor's season tickets. The neighbor got them in a divorce settlement... can I make this up? The Army parachuted on the field before kickoff during the first playoff game. There have been no fly-overs yet, but one of the dads sent us an email wanting to charter a jet for the state game that year in San Antonio. People around here think this is normal. It is a veritable cult. And we were delighted participants.

As you might assume, this was quite an upscale suburb. We were hanging on at the periphery. The senior student parking lot was filled with Jaguars, Porches, BMWs, and Audis.

Jeff: *I don't have to go to the auto show this year. I'll just drive over to the high school.*

THE SECRET TO HAPPINESS IS LOW EXPECTATIONS

We had to manage *expectations* for the boys when they got their permits.

David, a few months away from his driver's license, put 3,000 combined miles on our cars with us in the passenger seat. (*"Mom, just relax, you don't have to do anything."*) What he didn't realize at the time was he was about to be his brother's chauffeur. That is the bonus of having two kids. David thought we were underprivileged because we had no caller ID or DSL and drove used cars.

Greg was always a mommy's boy. He would tell me when I looked tired and when I looked beautiful. He bragged about my cooking and would let me know when my favorite TV shows were on. Greg played football too, but his intensity was a bit different than David's. He fancied himself *"A ladies' man."* The doorbell rang and there were six little blonde things on our porch. He came home two hours later. *"I hope you were a gentleman,"* I said. *"I didn't hear any complaints,"* said the ladies' man. Jeff started calling Dr. Joyce to stockpile penicillin. Greg was getting 105 on advanced Algebra tests. A sharp, logistical mind with reasoning skills way beyond his age. Jeff announced a performance bonus he got at work. *"Is that gross or net?"* asked Greg.

At fourteen and sixteen, the boys' conversations were completely comprised of movie dialog. They would repeat lines of every movie they had ever seen. Greg used this recall ability to his advantage in math and science. David never made that connection. He lost his backpack, wallet, homework, and football pants on a regular basis.

But he never misplaced his car keys. Soon after we gave him Jeff's old Explorer, he hung blue plastic bull testicles on the trailer hitch and fuzzy dice on the rear view mirror. He parked it next to a Mercedes at the high school. The first day he had the car he came running down the stairs: *"I have to drive Greg to Kroger. He's out of Q-Tips."* I couldn't wipe the smile off my face. No more carpooling. Once it was established that he was a pro, David taught Greg the rules of the road. *"It is courteous to go ten miles over the speed limit, so you don't slow people down."* And, *"Yellow lights really are like light green. So go."*

David needed gas money. He got a job with a landscape company. I know they paid the boy, but there was never any money by the time he pulled into the garage. Another difference between the boys.
David's going out.
Me: *You need money?*
David: *Yes.*
Me: *Here's $20.*

Me going out.
Greg: *Mom, do you need money?*
Where was Greg getting the money?? I'll tell you where.

One summer day we were over at my dad's house. The kids loved going into the attic. They each came home with a box. Greg also came home with a fan.

"Why do you need a fan?" I asked. *"Your brother is the one who is always hot."*

"I know," he said.

The next day Greg sold the fan to David for $25.

David had a boom box. Greg wanted one. David needed money. He offered it to Greg for $100. Greg got it for $10. *(*Greg: *"He kept following me around and lowering the price."*) Once they started to torture each other instead of us, Jeff and I knew we had done our job.

> **Sidebar:** Greg was always private.** He had a full size red locker in his room.**** In it he kept his valuables, money, Game Stop gift cards, photographs, affidavits…who the hell knows. A combination lock secured it. David cracked the safe one day. Greg will tell anyone with ears that David and I stole his stash of cash and bought him a birthday present with his own money. This is of course, preposterous, but repeated at every single family get together.

> ***Sidebar 2:** A couple years ago, I had to give my new 401K bank my beneficiary's Social Security numbers. I called David and he gave me his.
> David: *Have you called Greg yet?*
> Me: *No.*
> David: *It might be easier for you to get copies of Donald Trump's tax returns.*

> ****Sidebar 3:** Fast forward twenty years. David is getting married. His bride is Catholic. We are not. He needs his Baptism Certificate for proof he is a Christian or he cannot get married in her church. I know it is somewhere. We turn the house upside down. I find Greg's, Jeff's, and mine. No David. We contact the church where he was baptized. Apparently the pastor who was on deck back in 1990 had an issue with admin. There is no record of David.
>
> David: *I know where my baptism certificate is.*
> Me: *Where?*
> David: *In Greg's fucking locker. And he is going to sell it to me.*
>
> The priest at St. Rita's finally relents if we can find a *picture* of David being baptized. I found one. One.

Time traveling back…

Over the summer, David worked at the local country club in outside services. Seven dollars per hour plus tips and all you can eat. I felt like I got a raise. Aunty Joanna told him, *"Don't come home till you are full."* He really made $30 an hour if you count the food.

When he wasn't working he was busy cutting hair for tips. The entire defense was treated to buzz cuts at La David's Salon. Soon the players' little brothers were lining up. I was on the line calling the plumber every three weeks to get the team's hair out of the bathroom drain.

College prep meant taking the SAT which turned out to be a four-letter word. No sections in tackling, interceptions, or fumble recoveries, so we were in trouble. I signed up through the College Board for David to practice the SAT "questions of the day" on email. *"If John's hair is 4.5 inches longer than Jack's hair, how tall is Jack?"* Okay. I made that one up, but here is a real one:

Every student who studies art in a certain school receives exactly one of the grades A, B, C, or D. If 1/5 of the students receive A's, 1/4 receive B's, 1/2 receive C's, and 10 students receive D's, how many students in the school study art?

We hired a tutor the next day. Thank God I got my degree back when I knew something.

But the season that put me over the edge was David's senior spring. His heart was set on playing linebacker for a Division I school. I uncovered a new Axis of Evil on a plaque: *"If it involves tires, testicles, or technology, it's going to be a problem."* In the case of David's football highlight tape, we had two of three. There was a four-week period where the DVD wouldn't copy, the CD came back blank twice, the VHS copied to a DVD but stopped in the middle…When it was finalized we noticed David's name was misspelled on the DVD cover. I could go on. A fellow football mom, Laura, offered to do an "off the hook" recruiting package. There was one day when I had to go through a thousand pictures and newspaper articles for Laura while David was in the den watching *It's a Wonderful Life*. The twenty packages were finally mailed. Later I learned that instead of testing each DVD like I asked to be sure they all worked, David just played two out of the middle and figured they were all fine. Then he went off to lift weights. *"Everything is going to be fine, Mom. You'll see."* One time I tried to have a deep discussion with him. He said, *"Mom, everything you are telling me? I know it already."* Confidence and self-esteem were never an issue.

As you might *expect*, David was highly recruited. Plenty of colleges were looking at him. Unfortunately, most were beauty schools, but we knew once that highlight tape got into the right hands, the phone would ring for sure. According to David there were two places he wouldn't go – Notre Dame or anywhere in Michigan. He remembered wanting to shoot himself at Notre Dame's cathedral while during a visit Jeff spent three hours talking about the evolution of church design. And Michigan was *"too close to Canada."* Don't ask. And yet, with all the talk of state championships, SAT's, and colleges I heard David say over senior year Thanksgiving, *"Hey, Greg, do you ever just feel like building a fort?"*

Speaking of Greg, when he wasn't busy changing the combination to his locker, he started a lawn mowing business with two buddies. Which was quite lucrative as evidenced by a locker full of cash. After work he was a popular tutor with the girls.

"What are you tutoring them in?" I asked. *"Anatomy,"* he says and smiles. On a trip to the Dallas Aquarium, they brought disposable cameras to take pictures they would later draw of sea life. When I got the pictures developed it went like this: girl, fish,

girl, girl, fish, girl, fish. He got 105 in sophomore Geometry as a freshman and straight A's in junior Algebra as a sophomore. We were never worried about Greg's college prospects, as long as he didn't apply to an "all-girls" school.

~ ~ ~ ~ ~

I hate to admit I rolled my eyes when Dawn was sobbing on her front lawn after Paige went away to OU. And Andrea warned me how stressful it was with Nick. And Gabby ran around like a mad woman for Morgan. Then I got David's senior picture and starting crying. I cried when he walked to the center of Texas Stadium for the coin toss. I cried when I hung up his letterman's jacket. I cried while I drove to school delivering the homework he forgot. How can I let him go? And Greg is right behind him. There's only one solution. <u>I am going to home school the boys for college.</u> I was missing them, and they hadn't even left yet.

I knew I would miss all their buddies too. Tre would call David early in the morning looking for boxer shorts. Robert would be on our balcony getting a buzz cut and then chase me with fistfuls of hair. The last week of school, Luke sat at my breakfast bar at 6:45 a.m., while I made lunches in my robe with my hair in a clip. *"You know, Miss Isabel, you being fifty is crazy. You look thirty-two."* Luke can come over and take the stereo equipment for all I care.

Incredibly, David was accepted at the university of his dreams and made the Division I team as a walk-on linebacker. It all worked out. Just like he said.

After David left for college, Greg got involved in the high school film class. It was the school's version of *SNL* skits. The topics would be things like prom, spring break, baseball season starting, graduation…you get the picture. The boys would come over and gather props. Things like blow dryers, hats, makeup, and glasses would go missing. Sometimes they would film in the dining room – all you would hear is howling. These films would be played right before school started each morning. So creative and funny, Greg and his buddies became instant celebrities.

When it was Greg's turn to apply to the university (where David was) he wrote, directed, produced and starred in a video as part of his application. He faced a mirror and put on various rival school's t-shirts and made snide comments about each. At the end, he wears the university's shirt and declares it "a perfect fit." It brought the house down. He was not only accepted, the video was such a hit, it is shown every year at orientation.

Fast forward, Greg goes on to get a double degree in business. In his senior year, the boy who needed an interpreter as a toddler won first prize in a speaking contest at the business school. This got him an audience with the board of directors of the university—C-Suite leadership of organizations based in DFW. One of the board members hired him on the spot. Presto--his career as a consultant began.

THE SECRET TO HAPPINESS IS LOW EXPECTATIONS

As radio icon Paul Harvey used to say…"*And now you know the rest of the story.*"

> **Sidebar:** Sometimes a moment will stick in your mind forever. We were driving home from the lake. The kids are 10 and 12. The ride was 90 minutes, so we had time for conversations.
> Jeff: *What do you boys want to be when you grow up?*
> David: *A football player.*
> Greg: *I want to own a business.*
> Jeff: *What kind of business would that be?*
> Greg: *I don't know. But it will be a brother business.*

The two of them. The most *unexpected* gifts of all.

~ ~ ~ ~ ~

And if you have read this far and not considered making an appointment to get your tubes tied, I tip my hat to you – parenthood is not for the faint of heart. Despite your best efforts, kids keep it real whether you want to or not. In the 1970s, Erma Bombeck wrote a book entitled *Aunt Erma's Coping Book – How To Get From Monday To Friday…In 12 Days*. So, you see, it's always been like this. Exhausting, hilarious, challenging and ultimately satisfying in the most *unexpected* and arbitrary ways. The irony of it all is that while you think you are molding and shaping and raising them, they are having the exact same impact on you. It is a two-way street. Afterward, you are not the same. They have left their mark. And if you are very lucky you will one day say, "*I hope to grow up to be just like them.*"

They shoot horses, don't they?

"I'm a junkie for exhaustion, and I'm a junkie for setting up my expectations too high and then trying to meet them."
– Stephen Colbert

"Spirituality emerged as a fundamental guidepost... the deeply held belief that we are inextricably connected to one another by a force greater than ourselves – a force grounded in love and compassion."
– Brené Brown

At the end of the Lake House 1.0 chapter, I mentioned a detour...

It was another one of those if-I-can-just-make-it-through-this-week weeks. Or maybe whiplash from two sustained years of madness piling up on me. At work, managing two territories until The Corporation could find a suitable candidate to replace a guy who left, plus two houses, two kids, two dogs. Too much. I had been having a recurring daydream about being in a minor car accident with no injuries, and told I have to stay in the hospital for "observation".

It doesn't take a licensed therapist to know that is a dangerous escape fantasy. I needed to make an appointment with a shrink. But I figured that since I had identified what was wrong, I didn't need put yet another hour on my calendar to hear what I already knew – I was exhausted.

That week I was in three cities in four days and home just in time to pack because we invited our neighbors and their two boys to the lake house for the weekend. And it looked like rain. Which potentially meant four young children and four adults trapped in a tiny A-frame house.

I would find some way to pull it together, but my mind was already on next week. More travel, more deadlines and it was July 11. That meant I only had two weeks to plan Greg's seventh birthday party. I hated children's birthday parties. Everything about them. Especially the children. In our neighborhood, parties were elevated to a peculiar art form. You had to keep up. Bounce houses and arcades were so "last year." Now we were into live animals, magicians, renting out movie theaters, touring Cowboy stadium...you get the picture. Maybe I could find that magician to make it all disappear.

But first I had to take a shower. The guests were almost here. I vividly remember the prayer I said in that shower...*Oh God.*

THE SECRET TO HAPPINESS IS LOW EXPECTATIONS

I am headed for a brick wall. Everything is out of control here and it is speeding up. Please help me slow down. I need to slow everything down.

This would be the part in the movie where the scary music starts.

The neighbors arrived. The sun came out. They brought a snow cone machine. We launched the boat. The kids went tubing around the lake. Everything was going to be just fine. On the way back to the house some rain clouds were rolling in. (By the way, that's called "foreshadowing".) I jumped into the lake to ski a final lap to the dock.

And that is when Jesus took the wheel.

No one is exactly sure what happened next, except I fell. Spectacularly. As Jeff brought the boat around I couldn't feel my right leg. The men pulled me into the boat. After we docked they carried me to the house. I knew enough not to put any weight on it. Off we went to the regional lake hospital while the neighbors watched the kids.

I'll pause here to have you imagine what goes on in the emergency room of a lake hospital. It is a MASH unit. I joined a curious group of people with different parts of their bodies wrapped in makeshift bandages and towels. As Jeff settled me into a corner with my leg resting on another chair, I looked over his shoulder, out the window, to see a couple coming up the sidewalk. The man was being held up by his wife, holding a Dixie Cup over his eye.

This was a 911. Not for the man. For Jeff. Jeff has always had an eye phobia. It is so bad; he cannot watch cataract commercials or use eye drops. His last eye exam they did that puff test for glaucoma, and he wouldn't let them do the other eye. He said he'd take his chances. The rest of the exam was postponed because he could not stop tearing up looking at all the machines.

Back to the emergency room...I tell Jeff, *"Don't look."* He looks. Sees the man with his eye in a cup, grabs the armrests and starts rocking back and forth, chanting, *"No, no, no..."* He only snapped out of it when they called my name.

They took an X-ray and then put me in a bay sectioned off with curtains. There was a brief snafu when the doctor came in and asked how long ago I had my hysterectomy. *Oh. Wrong room.* Meantime, I hear one doctor call out to another: *"Hey, Bob. Come look at this."* I was hoping it was the X-ray of the guy with one eye. It wasn't. It was me. Apparently everything from just below my right knee to my ankle was shattered. Now it was starting to hurt. They gave me a brace and some crutches and told me to get to Dallas sooner than later for treatment. And do not put any weight on the leg.

David was nine at the time. When he was six, he met his best friend for life in first grade. That best friend had a mother who is a family doctor. Dr. Joyce and I met because of our boys and became fast friends. She naturally became our family doctor, and over time, one of my best friends. I had the lake hospital send Joyce the X-ray. She called back a little too fast — even before we got home from the lake. It's serious. She is recommending a surgeon she knows who is a leg wizard to put me back together. His name is Dr. Gilberg. And don't put any weight on the leg.

It is not lost on me that my whole life could have changed were it not for the coincidence of two kids who met in first grade.

Dr. Gilberg's office saw the X-ray and called me first thing Monday morning to come in. He examined my leg.

Doctor: *How good of a water skier are you?*
Me: *Apparently not that good.*
Doctor: *What did you hit?*
Me: *Nothing.*
Doctor: *It looks like you fell out of a seven-story building and landed on your leg.*
Me: *Can you fix it?*
Doctor: *I'm not sure.*

He explained it was a compound fracture with multiple cracks around the tibial plateau. That is the area under the knee. Said it was, "Cracked like an egg." Below that were several more breaks. It would require extensive surgery and a long recovery. Worst case I would be in a wheelchair. Best case I would have a slight limp. WHAT?
He scheduled surgery for the next week because we needed to let the swelling subside. I needed to let the panic subside. His PA walked me and Jeff out. He sensed my anxiety. Probably because I was sobbing. "*Listen, don't worry. He is the best. He is going to figure it out and you are going to be fine.*"

I hoped God was listening again.

Back at the ranch, things were indeed slowing down. A halt might be a better description. I was on the sofa or in bed. Jeff was a single dad. But if there was ever a silver lining, Gabby was now in charge of Greg's birthday party.

A funny thing happened on Day 3 while waiting for surgery on Day 10. I felt wired, tired, shaky, and queasy. It was so disturbing I called the doctor's office. The PA called back. He explained that I was having an adrenalin withdrawal because of being confined and immobile. He said adrenalin had the same effect on the body as cocaine and I was "detoxing". *"In that case, I have been high all my life,"* I told him.

Meantime, it wasn't the pain or the sofa that bothered me as much as the lack of privacy. I am very private. Even after almost twenty years of marriage, I always locked the bathroom door.
Flashback:
David (five years old): *Daddy, does Mommy make poopers?*
Jeff: *If she does, only dogs can hear it.*
David: *Does she poop?*
Jeff: *No. That's why she's so mean.*

So having someone near or in the bathroom because of my leg having to be in a certain position was beyond uncomfortable. I told Jeff I would probably have to divorce him after I healed because all the magic was gone.

THE SECRET TO HAPPINESS IS LOW EXPECTATIONS

Two days before the surgery, Dr. Gilberg calls me to tell me he is delaying my surgery by another couple of days because he wants to switch me to a brand new hospital. He felt more comfortable with a virgin operating room since my bones would be exposed for hours and that meant less chance of a bone infection. Fine. So now I not only had wheelchairs to worry about, but amputation.

The day of the surgery came. I was surprisingly calm. Either my adrenalin had all evaporated or I was starting to surrender – neither were familiar.

I woke up to a smiling Dr. Gilberg. Seven hours, six screws, and three plates and he had successfully put the jigsaw puzzle together. Now for the recovery. Five months. Basically, on my back. This would be interesting since I cannot even sit through a movie.

~ ~ ~ ~ ~

For the first time in my life, I had no choice but to relinquish the illusion of control. Truth is, I fancied myself to be "God's Assistant". I thought I was being benevolent in releasing God. My inner voice went something like this: *"Go help the people who need You – I've got this."* They say some folks get a God "whisper" or a "wink". Evidently, He decided I needed an anvil upside the head to understand Who was in charge. The message was about to be received loud and clear. God was in the process of "helping" me to discover how to let go of the delusion of self-sufficiency.

At the time, my job was commission-based. But The Corporation not only put me on paid disability, but also shifted my customers to a remote angel at corporate headquarters named Mike who handled my people so well, my only worry was they would forget me altogether. The next worry was the children. I could direct traffic at home, but who would shepherd them to their games, after school activities, and those godforsaken birthday parties? I'm ashamed to admit that all the stay-at-home moms who often made me roll my eyes, came to the rescue in spades. They actually got the kids to every event on time – sparing them running through parking lots with their mother in high heels perpetually fifteen minutes late. The next worry was Jeff. He had a demanding job and now had full custody. As David said years later… *there was a whole new chapter about to be stapled behind the Book of Revelations.*

One night around eight p.m. …
Jeff walked in from the garage. Disheveled. Tie undone, grocery bags in one hand, dry cleaning in another, and briefcase under his arm.

Kids: *Daddy, are we having dinner tonight?*
Jeff: (slamming cabinet doors) *I've been working ALL DAY, then had to pick up dry cleaning and go to Kroger and I CAN'T DO EVERYTHING AROUND HERE.*
I shrunk onto the sofa, ashamed of how satisfied I felt. Point made. Point taken.

THE SECRET TO HAPPINESS IS LOW EXPECTATIONS

We had to do something about running the household.

Enter Gabby. Next up in a series of angels. There is nothing Gabby relishes more than taking charge. And no one better at it. She marched into our Dallas office, stapled a calendar to the wall in the breakroom and began galvanizing the troops in a manner that made the Normandy invasion look like kindergarten. Keep in mind, this was a generation before Uber Eats and Door Dash. We thought drive-throughs were a big deal. So, every weekday *for months*, someone from my office would come around noon. They would feed me lunch, unload the dishwasher, put away laundry, let the dog out, set dinner in the fridge, and go back to work. Sylvie came with casseroles for the week. "*I'm Jewish. We love suffering.*" Gift cards appeared in our mailbox.

It was, in essence, a version of Habitat for Humanity, turned inside out. My co-workers and friends weren't building a house; they were organizing one while a soldier was down.

Now that I had little to worry about, I turned to the business of recovery. Shortly after I was sent home, a machine called a CMP arrived. Pretty sure it was an acronym for some medieval torture device. Its purpose was to continually bend my leg at increasing degrees to improve my range of motion. The goal was to go from "stiff" to ninety degrees, while on my back in bed. *Eight hours per day for six weeks. Can you imagine? No. You cannot.* Thankfully, the first two weeks I was on narcotics with the exception of one day when I decided to stop taking them because I wasn't in any pain. If you are following this at all, the reason I was not in pain was because of the narcotics. There was a gruesome twelve-hour period where I had to wait for the narcotics to kick back in after stopping. So, don't try that at home.

Finally, the six weeks was up, and I had enough range to advance to the next round of physical therapy. Two men came to pick up the machine. I heard Jeff talking to them in the foyer.
Jeff: *Please don't take it. It's the only time she's ever moved in bed.*
Which is a complete lie.
I let him have his laugh.

I "graduated" from the perpetual motion machine to water therapy. Marie next door told me I could use her pool for some of my PT. So, I hobbled over there every day to break up scar tissue by bending my leg on the steps in the pool. Not pleasant. But then I would float. In late September, she asked where I got such a great tan. "*Your pool,*" I said.

The PT was no picnic, but without the stress of work or kids or household, and a late summer tan, I was a new woman. My internal metronome was reset to forty beats per minute. Such stillness. I could actually inhale and exhale. Those outside my bubble, however, seemed to be rushing, hurrying, shouting. Strange.

People who visited would say, "*You've never looked better.*" Then Jeff would come down the stairs. Their reaction was an immediate, "*Oh.*" Jeff looked terrible. So did Gabby. Haggard. Apparently all the stress I was releasing found a new home.

Which is why when a national sales meeting in Atlanta was announced for mid-October, Jeff was extra enthusiastic about me attending. The doctor said it would be fine, as long as I was in a wheelchair. My good friend Suzanne from Houston was my territory partner for work. She became my shepherd. Meeting us at DFW, she remembers Jeff pushing my wheelchair toward her with such velocity that it rolled past three gates, and when she grabbed it, she turned around, and he was gone.

~ ~ ~ ~ ~

At the resort, The Corporation made sure we were in adjoining rooms so she could take care of me. That first night, we decided to celebrate my being away from the house for the first time in months. After dinner, Suzanne got a bottle of wine and brought it to the room. I didn't think it mattered to mention the two Tylenol PMs I just took. When the wine was gone, she tucked me in, and I passed out.

It was midnight when the fire alarms went off. For real. Full and immediate evacuation. The intercoms were blaring, doors were slamming, sirens wailing. The kitchen was ablaze. I was in a PM coma, asleep in my going-to-a-meeting-negligee, when Suzanne burst into my room in her robe, trying to dress me and get me in my wheelchair. She said it was like wrestling a limp octopus. But she exaggerates. On the way out she had secured both our purses in cross-body fashion. However, as she pushed me through the door, they got caught on the doorknob and she was snapped backwards, with the straps around her neck, brought to her knees. Practically strangled.

We were the last to make it out of the hotel and are greeted by the entire division of the company, standing in their pajamas and robes in the entrance courtyard. I am furious because not only am I making a grand exit in a wheelchair, but Suzanne has wrapped me in one of her white cotton robes with tiny blue dots that made me look like an escapee from a mental institution. My peach silk robe that matched my negligee was in the closet, for god's sake. Suzanne parked me under a tree and walked over to a group of our co-workers to chat while the kitchen was hosed down.
I heard a hissing noise. The sprinklers were coming on. One was right under my chair. The other two were aimed at my face and the back of my head. By the time Suzanne heard me scream above the sound of the fire hoses, I was completely drenched. With the destruction of my professional image complete, we went back to our rooms.

The next day Suzanne had to "shower me" since I could not put my weight on my leg yet and showers are slippery. I was naked. She was wearing a magenta bathing suit, which was understandable except for the color, but also a rubber bathing cap with daisies on it. Sometimes I don't know what's the matter with her. She didn't know where to hold me. And I became a *slippery* "octopus".

THE SECRET TO HAPPINESS IS LOW EXPECTATIONS

Later, during the meeting the president of my division walked over.
President: *How is it going with Suzanne?*
Me: *We have to shower together.*
President: *Any issues?*
Me: *Yes. I think she is starting to like me, if you know what I mean.*
We got a snort out of that.

Home, and one more month to go until my legs would once again be under me. How humbling those months were. The woman who was so self-reliant that she thought she could help God save some time. To be made so completely vulnerable and exposed that it took everyone she knew to take care of her.

I couldn't help but think about what you say when you are behind the boat, on your skis, holding that rope, ready to take off.
Hit it.

And off you go, into whatever comes next. A metaphor for life. Maybe something you could never have *expected* or prepared for…you are suddenly the camel going through the eye of the needle. And isn't it extraordinary to have others pulling you through?

~ ~ ~ ~ ~

Epilogue:
I think about Dr. Gilberg often. Walking my dog, on the Stairmaster at the gym, clicking around in my high heels, skiing (yes), dancing with my son at his wedding. What would have

happened if he didn't do my surgery? Would I limp? Be in a wheelchair? An amputee?

Last year it was twenty-four years since my surgery. I called his office. Yes, he was in. I drove there and parked in the lot. I called again. *Is he available? I am an old friend.* Yes, in fifteen minutes. The nurse put me in an exam room. My heart was beating pretty fast. He opened the door, and I stood up.
Me: *Do you remember me?*
Him: (Pause) *Oh yes, I do.*
Me: *I wanted to tell you that I forgive you for not sending flowers on our twentieth anniversary a couple years ago. But we've got the twenty-fifth coming up.*
He laughed. "*Has it been that long?*"
Him: (thinking I had an appointment) *Are you feeling okay?*
Me: *Yes. I came to thank you. Thank you for saving my leg and my mobility.*
And then I started crying.
Me: *Was it as serious as you said?*
Him: *Yes, it was.*
I looked at him. He didn't look sixty years old yet. I did the math in my head.
Me: *Were you even out of medical school?*
We both laughed and I hugged him. Hard. I started walking away and looked back. He is staring at me, smiling but a bit confused. I guess no one ever stopped by to tell him he saved a life. ⋀

Let there be Light

*"When God closes a door he opens a window,
but the hallways are hell."*
– Anonymous

*"This too shall pass.
Now would be good."*
– Bumper Sticker

Just when you think you've got your arms around life, it comes undone. Sometimes dramatically. 2006 was like that.

According to the Chinese calendar, 2006 was the Year of the Dog. Good thing we had twelve years to prepare for the next one. Lily Tomlin once said, *"It is always darkest before it turns completely black."* This was the theme at our house that year.

A month prior to the New Year, Jeff was told by his boss to prepare for a *huge* promotion. All indications were that Mommy was not only going to get her Jaguar, but a new house with a pool and a study. The day after the realtor walked through our house in mid-January, Jeff came home at noon with a cardboard box. His entire department had been dissolved.

Me: *I guess we're not moving.*
Jeff: *Not to the neighborhood you want.*

Jeff's response to a crisis was to keep to himself. But I knew he was troubled when he created a matrix of all the light bulbs in our house by size, quantity, and location. For the next five months Jeff split his time somewhat equally between finding more things to put in a matrix, watching the *History Channel*, playing solitaire, and searching for a job.

Worth a mention, after deep personal and professional introspection, I decided in mid-2005 to quit The Corporation to become a freelance writer. For me, this was tantamount to jumping off a cliff. But I told myself, *"What's the worst that can happen?"* With Jeff doing so well at work, even if I failed, there was a net.

Now, there wasn't. Footnote: don't ever ask that question.

Jeff and I were now both "working from home". Togetherness is highly overrated. It was similar to the romantic notion of "family dinners". We tried that about once every three weeks to remind us why we don't.

It was imperative that Jeff find something. Soon would be good. The boys and I were very supportive.

THE SECRET TO HAPPINESS IS LOW EXPECTATIONS

David: *As long as there is no personal interview involved, dad should be fine.*

Then David made his father a CD. The title cut? *Get a Job.*

Greg: *"Next week is career day at school. Who do I bring?"*

After picking up some dry cleaning, I interrupt Jeff in yet another game of solitaire:
Me: *"Is this your white shirt or David's?"*
Jeff: *"Mine."*
Me: (pregnant pause) *"Do you think you will ever wear a white shirt again?"*
Jeff: *"Yes. At your funeral."*

Jeff is leaving for the airport to visit his folks in Chicago.
Me: *Do you have your keys?*
Jeff: *Yes.*
Me: *Driver's license?*
Jeff: *Yes.*
Me: *Phone?*
Jeff: *Yes. I've got everything. You only get one more question.*
Me: *Do you have a job?*

Severance was about to run out when our friend Craig came up with a brilliant idea. As a youngster Greg bore an uncanny resemblance to country music star Brad Paisley. Craig said if we really got desperate, we could put Greg in a cowboy hat, and I could write a paternity letter. Before I could put pen to paper – the phone rang. The job Jeff had been pursuing for three months looked like it was coming true. We had a close call when they asked him to take a personality test. *("Let me take it for you honey – I've got one.")* Having nothing left to prove in solitaire, Jeff took the job.

It was working for a retail development company. Privately held and very successful, they assisted retail clients in all aspects of store remodels, reconfiguration, and planning. Jeff knows real estate/construction better than anyone, but until he got into retail, he couldn't tell you the difference between Crate & Barrel and Abercrombie & Fitch. Something is not right when I am in front of a computer all day and he is running through malls. The first week his boss asked him to meet individually with about thirty-five people. When asked how that was going, Jeff presented The Boss with a human resource matrix he devised. If it is anything like the light bulb matrix, the man is still unfolding it.

At the time, after an inexplicable *unexpected* introduction, a good part of my fledgling business was affiliated with a woman named Karen, who founded a highly successful practice management firm in Chicago. She consults with physicians and surgeons throughout North America. Working with Karen is a lot like strapping yourself to a rocket. She caused me more sleepless nights than two newborns put together. Karen is a cross between Miranda in *The Devil Wore Prada* and Glenda the Good Witch in *The Wizard of Oz*. So, it's difficult.

Karen's problem was she had more confidence in me than I did. She hired me as a content writer, but soon I was being groomed as a speaker and consultant. She didn't waste any time throwing me in the deep end of the pool without a life preserver. *"You're doing great!"* she yells as I flail around gasping for breath. In 2006, we did seminars and consultations in Dallas, Las Vegas, Houston, Naples, LA, Chicago, and Columbia SC. She would assign me marketing communications work primarily with Plastic Surgeons and their staff with an occasional Orthopedic Surgeon thrown in. We spoke at packed workshops. Most of the time my heart was beating so hard I could hardly hear myself talk. What I really needed was to speak at a program for Cardiologists. At least I would have felt safe.

> **Sidebar:** I have to tell the Las Vegas story because I remember it like it was yesterday.
>
> Karen: (channeling her Miranda) *Isabel, we are going to speak in Las Vegas, and you cannot arrive looking like something out of* Little House on the Prairie.
>
> At first I was offended. I had a closet full of suits and high heels. But come to find out she was thinking something a bit flashier, which is less my style. She buys me a silver bolero jacket with rows of sequin flaps that looked like miniature mirrors. Then instructs me to find a white ribbed turtleneck, silver chain, tight black pants, and high-heeled boots. And a belt with an ornamental buckle. This all went into a suitcase I rolled into the Wynn. I was to be down in our ballroom with our audience by seven a.m. Sharp.

At 6:30 a.m., I put on my costume. I looked like a woman who goes to sleep at 6:30 a.m., if you know what I mean. Still dark. I looked down the corridor. No one. Good. I ran to the elevator. Nuts. Here comes a man in a suit. I stared straight at the elevator doors. I knew he was looking at me. He cleared his throat.

Man: *Do you have any idea what time it is?*
Me: *Oh, I know. I'm so embarrassed. My boss had me wear this because we are speaking to a group downstairs, and she wanted us to look like Las Vegas.*
Man: (tries to interrupt me) *Ma'am…*
Me: *I never ever dress like this, and I hope you don't think I came out of someone else's hotel room…at this hour.*
Man: *Ma'am. I forgot my watch. I simply wanted the time.*
The elevator doors opened. It was quiet all the way down to the lobby.

When it was my turn to speak at the conference, I did prepare a good opening line. *"I'd like to see Celine Dion's face when she finds out this is missing from her closet."*

~ ~ ~ ~ ~

So here we were mid-year, with Jeff happy at a new job, and me, starting to feel a new groove as an official "sole proprietor" of my own business.

As they say during the Ginsu Knives ad on late night TV: *But wait. There's more.*

At the lake house around the fourth of July, I found a lump. Of course, it would be nothing. I just had a mammogram in the spring. Only one percent of women under fifty have breast cancer. I've never even gotten the flu. Or allergies. Or headaches. Hives, occasionally, but that's on Karen.

The medical version of speed dating ensued. A month of doctor visits and testing smashed into two weeks. My radiologist actually gave me *adrenalin* during the biopsy (*Doctor, I am a donor.*) It was breast cancer.

This was beyond *unexpected*.

Minutes after I got the phone call, before I even could tell Jeff, Dawn came over to pick up Greg for practice. I am in tears. I tell her it is serious.

Dawn: *Why are you crying? What's wrong?*
Me: *I have breast cancer.*
Dawn: *Oh, I thought maybe you were pregnant.*

I stopped crying. We figured if it was caught early enough, I would be clear in five years. Children are around your neck forever. Dawn had a point.

I didn't tell many people at first. Probably because it would threaten my state of denial. Ultimately, there is no way out. You have to surrender to the diagnoses. I felt deeply diminished. Damaged. Labeled. The whole idea of being part of some pink ribbon club, running around in a turban filled me with rage. Oddly, death never entered my mind. But darkness certainly fell around me.

They say there are stages of grief. I got stuck on – and remain to this day – in the anger phase. I took it personally and have never been able to feel the way I once did about my body. Something died on July 11 when I got that call. Remember when I broke my leg in pieces? That was also July 11. Believe me, it is circled on my calendar. Breaking my leg was bad enough. But that was skeletal. This was systemic. I literally felt something shatter inside of me. It was the security I had always had about my perfect health. Gone.

There is no history in our family, and even if there was, less than twelve percent of breast cancers are genetic. Research lists dozens of attributes that contribute to being a woman at high risk. I have none of them. It was a lightning strike. Lucky me. I would have preferred the winning lottery ticket.

After a month of keeping my "secret", little by little I let friends know. They rallied around in spite of me. My friend's husband Dennis called reminding me he gives oral breast exams, but for therapeutic purposes only. *"You are forbidden from enjoying it."* Jeff waited in the hall during my contrast MRI where they shot blue dye in my veins. When I came out he asked me how long my face would be tinted blue, and would they give me something for that? As Karen would say, these men are listed under the category of *not funny*.

After the initial bad news everything got significantly better. I had the least aggressive, smallest, most retarded form of breast cancer. "*Garden variety*" said the oncologist. No nodes involved. Small lumpectomy. Seven weeks of radiation and I am considered "cured". For me, breast cancer was and is more a mental illness. Even today, I'm literally terrified of going to a doctor for the most routine checkups, thinking they will find something. I will always have to check a box that says "Cancer."

People ask, *"How are you different?"* Truthfully, it didn't change my perspective on life one bit. I never took my health for granted. That wasn't a revelation. But *"If I can just make it through this week..."* was more of a prayer for a while. At times when I was the most scared, a stranger would say something, billboards I passed would have words I needed to see, a song would play. *You're fine, you've got this, all will be well.* They say if you watch and listen, you experience "God winks."

Curiously enough, on one of my bad days, I had a spiritual experience at the car wash. Next to the funny cards was a book rack. There it was – *Just Enough Light for the Step I'm On*.

Isn't that all we ever need? Knowing that you only have to take one step at a time. And the Light will always be nearby. This week and always.

Lake House 2.0

"I've enjoyed as much of this as I can stand."
– Bill Anderson, 1962 Country Music Song

"For every financial windfall, an equal unexpected cost."
– The Law of Household Economics

We sold the first lake house the month after my water skiing accident. A year later, in August 2000, we bought another one because there was way too much money in the bank. The house was small and needed work, but we compromised to afford something on open water. Figured we would "fix it up" along the way. All the repairs we anticipated making in the first five years happened in the first five months. So what. All that is forgotten while sitting on the porch in a rocker overlooking Cedar Creek Lake.

One incident we won't soon forget is the boat starting on fire in the middle of the lake over that first Labor Day. There is something counter-intuitive about being surrounded by water and dousing flames.

My famous line, *"Jeff, should we use the emergency flares?"*

"I think the four stories of black smoke is enough," he replied.

~ ~ ~ ~ ~

It was an escape in every sense of the word. And by that I mean a haven for friends and family. Jeff and I had to go back to work on Mondays just to regain our balance. Despite the repairs and assorted surprises, it was a perfect place to entertain. Jeff dragged the kids behind the boat on tubes, skis, kneeboards, and wakeboards. And when you drag a boy behind a boat all day, you know exactly where they are that night. I kept the oven at 400 degrees for bagel bites and pizza rolls, washed towels, and stood on the porch yelling, *"STOP DIVING off the boathouse roof."*

Apart from the snake Jeff shot out of the boathouse, children visiting for the weekend without their ADD medicine, and the boat almost sinking, it was a relatively quiet first season. Which was good because in the winter before the second season we decided to turn the garage into a den. This investment was predicated on the commission check I would be getting for a huge sale I made that would cover the whole cost. The order was manufactured and ready to ship and invoice, right as the carpet was being laid in the new den. But wait a minute. My customer was facing some stockholder issues. Cancelled the order.

THE SECRET TO HAPPINESS IS LOW EXPECTATIONS

"This never happens." Well, the "new addition" was ready to be born, so we had an extra room and a payment plan.

Summer came. Time to christen the season with a big party. The adults had just as much fun as the kids. A bunch of friends and family were on their way to the lake. My mother- and father-in-law were with us. Mom answered the phone while I was on the dock and came to tell me, "Amy called, and she and Keith want you to know they are bringing down the jet skis." "Great," I said. So they came and Jeff helped get them in the water – we had a ball. When the party was almost over my mother-in-law said how lovely it all was, however, she had been introduced to everyone but the Jetskis. You know, the Polish couple that Amy and Keith brought. Oh.

Jeff got a great bonus. We put part in a savings account for our own jet skis. As soon as we saved enough, our sea wall collapsed. It cost thousands, but the alternative was watching our property fall into the lake. We decided we are not saving money anymore because every time we do...something big breaks. Incidentally, that same year our next door neighbor's sea wall also collapsed. The next thing we know, he is in a scout master uniform with a dozen boy scouts all tasked with earning a "rebuilding a sea wall badge." We watched from our porch with a mixture of shock and awe.

The next year Jeff volunteered to host his dojang's annual Karate party at the lake. In the long run, I would have preferred he swap his black belt for a scout uniform. Anyway, thirty Karate people came. We planted the flag of South Korea on our lawn and let the fun begin. We started out with two jet skis, a boat, and two toilets. At the end of the day only one worked. And it wasn't the toilets. (My friend Suzanne warned me our neighbor, Larry, had a roof that pointed at our house like a poisoned arrow. *"Bad Feng Shui,"* she said.) In total surrender, we replaced the Korean flag with a plain white one. Jack-the-boatman, the septic guy and a plumber joined us. Larry, our friend with the "arrow", opened his bathrooms until the septic was drained. So technically we had thirty-four people at the party. We found out our boat was dead, and a new Jet Ski engine was on the list. "Boat" was supposed to be in the 2007 Matrix and the jet skis were just acquired (on schedule) in March. Jack did come through with a real honey of a used boat. At the time, we considered turning our den into a bedroom for Jack. Mutual convenience. I kept a framed photograph of Jack on our mantle with a candle next to it. Not kidding.

In case you are thinking it was all parties and potties, it was not. Occasionally we had a day alone – just the four of us where 'the school of life' was in session. In 2004, the boys' sex education got a boost. Two of the neighbor's dogs got swept up in a romantic interlude and got stuck. They were howling.
Me: *Jeff, come out here and get these dogs apart.*
Jeff: *Just leave them alone, they'll relax and be fine in a few minutes.*
Then the boys heard them, and subsequently, saw them. They were horrified.
David: *Dad! Come here and help these dogs, they're crying and can't get apart from each other.*

It took twenty-five minutes. I know because I was on the porch with my sons. When it was over I looked at them. *"That can happen to you, too."* Their eyes got really big. It was a Hallmark moment.

Speaking of dogs, no one had more fun at the lake than Tanner and Champ. Tanner never understood he couldn't make it across the lake, so we had to keep him leashed even in the water. He swam the length of the English Channel with Jeff holding him on a light leash next to the boat house. Champ on the other hand would retrieve tennis balls for hours until we passed out. When Gabby brought Parker, her golden retriever, he preferred to lay on the raft and float. It was a spectacle.

You will remember me mentioning that in 2005, it was (what I *expected* to be) my final day in Corporate America. I officially began my freelance writing business. Karen, who on any given day would claim to be *busier-than-the-New York City-police-department*—kept me in a perpetual whirlwind. Despite the high anxiety she triggers inside me, I will always consider her my mentor and "fairy godmother." Karen is big on parties, special events and epic celebrations.

Sidebar: On the twentieth anniversary of her thriving practice management business, Jeff and I were invited to a weekend in Chicago commemorating the occasion featuring dinner on Michigan Avenue, an architectural walking tour near Lake Shore Drive, and an evening of fireworks off Navy Pier aboard the former Presidential Yacht. For real. In New York during one of our workshops, Karen and I stayed in Times Square, went to a private party in Greenwich Village and dined at Joe Allen's in the theatre district. Back in Chicago she invited me to a party of twelve held at a jewelry store on Oak Street for a black tie dinner. Earlier in the day the women got to choose jewelry from their cases. I was wearing a pair of earrings that cost more than my house. As we arrived past the armed guard at the door, a set of twins were playing harps and a butler was serving French 75s from a silver tray. I am not making this up.

Footnote: Karen is listed in the Social Register of Chicago. This is synonymous with knighthood. Once, I made the mistake of referring to her as "a Registered Socialite." She was not amused. Apparently, they are not the same.

You may be wondering, *"How does one repay such generosity?"* Hang on. In early August, Karen decided we should have a meeting to discuss future marketing plans. *"Come to the Lake House for the weekend,"* I-said-and-would-later-curse-myself. Karen arrived and for exactly five hours nothing bad happened. That evening Karen went into the kitchen and discovered an inch of water covering the entire house. The toilets were flooding. *Oh my God!* I screamed and grabbed some towels.

Karen: *Dearie, there is six inches of water in here. We'll need more than a towel.*

THE SECRET TO HAPPINESS IS LOW EXPECTATIONS

I ran to Larry's in my pajamas, and he stayed till midnight with his WetVac. As he should, since it is his arrow, after all… He summoned the septic guy to return. I did not sleep well. The next day we thought we were fixed up and twenty-four hours later Jeff, the kids, my sister and the dogs arrived. Everything seemed under control until the tuna steaks. Jeff made his special basil pesto marinade. Two hours later Karen took a shower and emerged with pesto up past her ankles. I have been on trips with her where she doesn't even like to remove her shoes at the airport. *I marinated my mentor.* She left the same day. I don't even remember slowing down to let her out at the airport.

So now we have a broken septic system. The lowest quote was $10,000 to replace it. My new theme song became, *"It's my potty and I'll cry if I want to."* For those of you unfamiliar with a septic system, it is basically comprised of a tank with legs like a spider underground. Jeff thought the main leg might be clogged. If he could somehow remove the clog, we might be able to save the system, our toilets, and the college fund. Jeff, David, and Larry went to work. They identified the pipes they needed to expose. David dug a hole the size of a Volkswagen.

One pipe was clogged, the other clear, so Jeff's theory was correct. I asked Jeff," *How did you know?*" "*It was a crap shoot,*" he said. Now, that's funny, I don't care who you are.

We also learned David is an awesome ditch digger. It was comforting to know, if he didn't get into the NFL, he had a trade.

Now everything was fixed. The boys' buddies came to the lake all summer long. The amount of food they ate never ceased to amaze. It was like the locusts in a Japanese horror movie. I was in heaven. Things got a little more interesting when the boy and girl parties started happening. By interesting I mean having a front row seat observing teenage girls, since I was lucky enough to sidestep that in real life.

One particular episode still makes me shake my head. The boys invited three girls down – all presumably getting ready to start college. One of the moms was nice enough to send a big tin of BBQ. On Sunday I went on the porch and asked if they would get the tin and warm it up while I made the salads.
Girls: *"What do you mean warm it up? Like in the microwave?"*
Me: *"NO. Like on the stove. Aluminum blows up in a microwave. Get a pan."*
Girls: *"We don't get it. Can it go in the oven?"*
Me: *"No, just put it on the stove in a pan."*
Girls: *"How high do we do the burner? Do we stir it? How do we know it's done?"*
It took three of them to warm up four pounds of beef in a skillet. These boys are in trouble if they think anyone besides their mothers will be feeding them in the future. Luke told me later that the girls went back to school and told their friends I was mean.

A weekend later Jeff and I were in Walmart in Gun Barrel City and saw the book *Pregnancy for Dummies* at the checkout. Jeff decided maybe a talk with the boys would be a good idea. He gathered them around the kitchen table and talked about sex, finances, working together, and finding a partner. Jeff could rent himself out for father-son talks…it would bring tears to your eyes. But then he blew it.

Greg: *Dad, what about all the hot girls? What do you do about them?*
Jeff: *Oh, you can have all the fun you want with hot girls, but when you're ready to settle down you want someone like your mother.*

Wait. *What?*

That was in July. In November, Greg told us he found his future wife.
"*She's perfect. She hates nuts, won't eat coconut, likes* Seinfeld, *and remembers the* Dinosaur *TV series.*"
I say, relationships have been built on much less.

The saga of 2006 followed us to the lake. Within a few months of Jeff being laid off, Tanner went missing at the lake and a day later I nearly totaled my company car.

Jeff: *"If my mother goes to jail, we are going to have a country music hit."*

Our hearts literally stopped when Tanner disappeared from the lake in June. So unlike him and we searched for hours. After three days, we went home without him. Larry would continue the search in our absence. Jeff was a wreck, and I laid in bed for two days with my insides shaking. I prayed harder than I can ever remember praying. A few days later we went down for fourth of July to visit the shelters and put up flyers. We even got the missing dog announced on the lake radio station. My brother, Caroline, and Steve were driving down. Believe it or not, Andrew stopped the car at the end of our street and Steve saw Tanner. Just sitting there waiting. Smiling like he'd been at vacation bible school for the week.

My prayers mirrored those I read in Anne Lamott's book, *Traveling Mercies*. She said her prayers are always the same. Either *"Please, please, please,"* or *"Thank you, thank you, thank you."* I promised God I would never forget that miracle. Tanner is on the other side of the rainbow bridge now, but I often think of that answered prayer with gratitude I cannot put into words.

Now that everyone was accounted for, we celebrated. As usual, everything is perfect until people arrive wanting to do something. One weekend in particular we put the jet skis in the water but it turns out the batteries were dead. Okay, we'll go on the boat. Uh oh. Someone left the boat fan on since last weekend. Battery? Also dead. Okay, let's eat. But Jeff cleaned the grill "really good" and knocked a tube loose and it melted all the knobs to the surface. I ran to Walmart to find batteries and buy sandwiches. While I was crawling around the automotive parts aisle with my glasses on, reading the battery charts, a man approached me. *"Excuse me ma'am, what aisle are the auto filters in?"*

He thought I worked there. At the Walmart. In Gun Barrel City. It actually stings to remember that.

THE SECRET TO HAPPINESS IS LOW EXPECTATIONS

On Memorial Day around 2007, one of our jet skis broke. Jeff brought it into a service center about thirty miles away. The short story? We didn't get it back until Labor Day. The long story? Jeff almost went to jail. The group that ran the place was so utterly incompetent that after hearing him on the phone with the repair guy, I went with him to get the ski so no one would get hurt. When we got there it turns out the engine now worked, but the seat on the ski was cracked. It was left out in the sun, and they blamed Jeff for the weather. There was a brief moment when Jeff's voice got really low, and he started backing away from the manager. Above Jeff's head was a sign that read, "Ammunition Sold Here". I pulled Jeff out of there just in time.

Turns out the dealer gave us an engine from a junkyard, but once we discovered that, we couldn't go back to complain because he closed up the Kawasaki shop and became the minister of Living Vine Church of Cedar Creek. Of course he did.

Fire ants ate the boat switch, so our boat was suspended for a while. Then came the drought. We have a whole lot more property now that there is no water in the lake. My favorite weekend of the summer? When our air conditioner broke in our real house, we went to cool off at the lake, only to find our A/C was broken there too. The fire ants that vacated the boathouse migrated to the air conditioner and stopped it up. We had a *For Sale* sign that went in and out of the closet.

~ ~ ~ ~ ~

If you think this is just a soliloquy about the Money Pit, you are dead wrong. To this day people talk about the lake house like it was Shangri-La. My girlfriend parties were legendary. It was the perfect hideaway. After the debacle with me driving the boat in Lake House 1.0, I declared our girlfriend weekends "engine free". Once you park in the driveway, you are not riding in another vehicle. This took away all the anxiety for me. Sometimes we didn't even use the grill. One eye was kept on the toilets, but that was manageable.

Two of the most popular themes were: *"If-he-doesn't-cut-it-out-I'm-leaving,"* and *"How-could-I-still-be-doing-this-for-a-living?"* We never really arrived at an answer, but no one went home until all the wine was gone.

We floated all day on innertubes and at night watched movies, played games, mixed drinks, made gourmet meals and danced to Bruno Mars. One of our popular guest stars was Carolyn, the masseuse I found at the lake who made house calls. She would set up a table in the back bedroom. It was fun to watch someone go in for a massage with Carolyn for the first time. They were not the same when they stumbled out. She was five-foot-three and weighed probably ninety-five pounds but had hands of steel. She was also a cross between a tarot card reader and a witch and would give you advice depending upon where she found knots on your body. Curiously, a lot of it had to with sex. The next morning we all felt like we were in a car accident the night before. It was fantastic.

After several memorable seasons, we lost Carolyn. She moved to Australia. Seems her "geographical astrologer" told her the man of her dreams was waiting in the Outback. This is a true story.

~ ~ ~ ~ ~

And then there was another theme. You've heard of "waiting to exhale?" This was more like "waiting to inhale." Gabby calls one fall day.
"Do you know what we've never done together?"
I didn't dare answer that one.
She continues…"*Smoke a doobie.*"
If you are confused, that is what people who remember Woodstock called a joint. *"We've never gotten high together."* Well, it wasn't like I was excluding her. I was around fifty at the time and only inhaled once in my thirties.
Me: *Where are you going to get the doobie?*
Gabby: *In my high heels at the top of the closet. The one Claire gave me for my fiftieth birthday. I've been saving it. Let's go to the lake and smoke.*

Off we went the next weekend. We had to be careful where we sat outside. Five doors down was the county sheriff. Lucky for us, the wind was going in the other direction toward the scoutmaster's house. They weren't home. We got into our chaise lounge chairs and lit up. After a while…
Me: *I don't feel anything, do you?*
Gabby: *No.*
Me: *Maybe it's old.*

Gabby: *Maybe.*
Me: *I don't feel anything.*
Gabby: *Me either.*
I think we said that about twenty times.
I was staring at the clouds. Gabby was quiet. This should have been my first clue. Then she went into the house. I lost track of time. Where was she? How long had it been? I got up to find her. Gabby is on my sofa with my Halloween candle between her legs. She is digging into the candle with her fingers and eating the decorative candy corn I put between the candle and the glass.
Me: *For god's sake, I have fresh candy corn in the pantry.*
Gabby: *But this is soooo warm.*
That Christmas our families got together and exchanged gifts. Gabby's girls were confused why I got her a candy corn candle instead of holly or peppermint. Gabby glared at me across the table. "*I got this one on sale,*" I said. That was fun.

But the real rip snorter was with The Grape Girls – Carrie, Marla, Abby, Meredith, Jackie, Jen, and Sam. This group banded together in 2002. We didn't all work at the same place, but we all worked in the same industry calling on the design community. All of us were reps for furniture, tile, textiles, carpet. Since we were not direct competitors, we often did presentations together and soon we scheduled group lunches. Always on Friday. Always at a restaurant on lower Greenville Avenue called The Grape. Hence, The Grape Girls were born. We would meet at noon and leave around 3:30, sometimes 4:00, when we'd be out of

THE SECRET TO HAPPINESS IS LOW EXPECTATIONS

stories and couldn't laugh any more, and probably should have called an Uber. But they didn't exist yet.

Years passed and sadly, The Grape closed. We found another restaurant that was BYOB because our "meetings" were becoming unaffordable. We are a unique group because no two of us are alike. A wide range of ages and backgrounds and lifestyles, but together we have a mysterious bond. We are ad hoc sorority sisters. After over twenty years together, we have seen each other through births, deaths, layoffs, marriages, divorces, moves, bad bosses, hospital stays, and raising kids. And lake house weekends.

The first time was pretty tame, except for Jen falling behind the recliner in a backwards somersault without spilling a drop of her margarita. Another weekend we mixed a few cocktails and rewrote the Pina Colada song: *"If you like Pina Coladas, standing out in the rain..."* Only our rendition was *"If you like bean enchiladas..."* Abby, Carrie, Sam, and Marla made up all new lyrics and the five of us sang in three part harmony at the top of our lungs. Too bad we didn't have a designated scribe. Trust me, it was Grammy worthy.

One of the more interesting episodes involved Carrie bringing cookies. Her husband is in a band and one of the members baked some special treats. The kind you don't smoke. No worrying about the wind. I was wearing a sweatshirt from the university where David played football. That will be important later. We put out the appetizers and the cookies and mixed the drinks and soon the eight of us were laughing until we were in tears on the patio. I had a grand total of half a cookie. Unbeknownst to me, ingesting weed is a lot stronger than puffing it. I went inside to check on dinner. Marla followed me. She had her phone. Sam and Meredith came in to toss the salad. I felt like Marla was secretly taking my picture. Soon I was convinced she was going to send a picture of me and my sweatshirt to David's coach, telling him I was "high" and get him kicked off the team. This all made perfect sense at the time.

Me: *I'm going to bed.*
Girls: *It's eight o'clock.*
Me: *I don't feel good.*
In fact, I was having a panic attack. Took Champ and shut the door and laid in bed. I was so scared. What if Marla sent my picture? What if I had brain damage? What would I tell the kids? I had to pray. "Our Father…" "Our Father who…" I couldn't remember the rest of the prayer. Jackie came to check on me. I heard her say, *"She's breathing. She's okay."* And I fell asleep.

The next morning I heard all about the party I missed. Sam and Carrie diagnosed me as paranoid. I promised to stick to Grey Goose from now on. I subsequently heard all of them had a couple cookies, but Jackie stole the show, eating six. Carrie went home and told her husband about the escapade. He was not amused. Told her we weren't supposed to put those cookies on a platter next to the charcuterie board. He did, however, declare Jackie an honorary member of the band.

Fast forward a couple years, another lake date. Coincidentally, Jen was just returning from Colorado and would be bringing gummies. She smuggled them in her *daughter's* purse. *(There is so much wrong with that.)* After floating and dinner, we broke out Crimes Against Humanity. Jen broke out the gummies. Jen and I were partners. At one point we got a card that said "tentacies." We had Sam look it up. Google never heard of it. Turns out when we put on our glasses, it said "testicles." And something about a pangender octopus. Maybe I am imagining all of this. But I do remember taking a pass on the gummies and when I went to the bar, there was a bottle of Grey Goose with my name taped on it. And it was sitting on top of a sheet of paper where Marla had printed out The Lord's Prayer. In large font.

~ ~ ~ ~ ~

Epilogue:
We sold the house after the divorce. (See "Starting Over. Late.") It was like losing a family member. Joanna thinks houses have hearts and souls. This one did. It was a jewel box. The wind chimes, the stereo blasting country musical all day and Andrea Bocelli on Sunday mornings. The smell of bacon and beer and taquitos. Red solo cups, coolers, and fireworks. I carried out the last moving box and heard the screen door slam behind me. I cried all the way back to Dallas. I knew deep down, there would never be another place on earth that would hold that many memories in my lifetime.

Years later David chose to have his bachelor party at Cedar Creek. The boys rented a house near our former homestead. All of them had grown up on that lake. Recently David told me he and Greg have been stalking the people who bought our house. They intend on buying it back from them some day. To be continued…

And just last week, twelve years since we sold the house, my brother sent me a photo by email. Subject line: "*I miss those times.*" I opened it up and it was a picture taken from the porch looking toward the lake. Jeff in the boat slip, girls floating, Gabby carrying a tray of food, dogs swimming, guys on the dock fixing something, and four boys diving off the boat house roof.

Starting Over. Late.

"In three words I can sum up everything I've learned about life: It goes on."
— Robert Frost

"Every new beginning comes from some other beginning's end."
— Seneca

Most couples who prefer to test drive their relationship will live together before deciding when and if they will get married. Jeff and I never had that option. With two sets of Roman Catholic parents, it was not only not an option, it wasn't even in the realm of possibility. However, living together *after* our marriage was over? That turned out to be distinctly possible.

The divorce was final in January and until the house was sold, there we were. For an *entire year*. All the chapters I had highlighted in my copy of *Codependent No More* were buried in the bottom of a moving box along with my soul, as I carried on with work, grocery shopping, cooking, holidays and birthdays. I drew the line at dinner parties.

We were playing house, alone/together. I told myself I was keeping things "normal" because it was Greg's senior year/first year of college. But that wasn't the only reason. Truth is, I was test driving being divorced. I knew that for me, the marriage was over. That didn't mean I let my mind wander too far into the future. Twenty-eight years. Done.

On the surface, we were the perfect couple. And our good times were absolutely genuine – they are what kept us going. We were meant for each other in so many ways. Like the Carly Simon song, we had our *"silent noons, tearful nights, angry dawns,"* as most couples do. However, there came a time when it was necessary for us each to go in different directions. Sadly, we lost each other along the way and that's a high price to pay. Today, we have found space for each other that remains amiable, and for that, I am forever grateful. That is all I will say about it.

I found myself in an "intermission" until the next act would begin.

Our house finally sold between Thanksgiving and Christmas. That same week, my realtor called. The perfect house just listed a few miles away. They were motivated sellers because they were going through a divorce. Strange. I guess they weren't keen on living together anymore. They accepted my offer.

THE SECRET TO HAPPINESS IS LOW EXPECTATIONS

Moving day was February 1. The new owners of our old house were moving in Feb 2. I'll take a brief pause here to mention the people who bought our house were despicable. Negotiations went on for weeks. Every time we gave in, they wanted more. Never in good faith. It continued after the closing – coming to a thundering crescendo the day I was supposed to move out. There was a matter of a once-in-a-hundred-year ice storm blowing through Dallas. My realtor called their realtor to request a two-day postponement due to "Acts of God." The request was denied. They wanted me to pay them the $400 per day in the contract for any delay. I filed that under "Acts of the Devil" as my baby grand piano was loaded into the truck. Although less than three miles away, it took an hour, one way, to crawl over the icy roads. Incredibly, everything eventually arrived in good shape.

Except for me.

But hang on. The phone rang. It was the Despicables. It was forty degrees in the house. Could I please turn on the heat for them? They accidentally put down the wrong start date and it was still under my name. They were freezing. *Hmmm. What a delicious turn of events.* I rolled it around my tongue for a few minutes. *Nope. Couldn't retaliate.* I called the energy company, and it was easily fixed with a phone call, but I did let them freeze for six hours. I called back the Despicables who barely managed to mumble a "thank you" before hanging up on me. Maybe their lips were blue.

A month after the boxes were unpacked and pictures were hung, I picked up the mail to learn my identity had been stolen. My American Express had a $12,000 balance. On top of everything else going on…how could this happen?

I grabbed my phone and dialed the fraud hotline. Jared answered.
Me: *Hello. My identity's been stolen. I don't know what to do. This never happened before.*
Jared: *Don't worry, we will close your account and report all fraudulent charges.*
Me: *I've never had a balance that high.*
Jared: *Let's go through each line item and you tell me which is accurate, and which is theft.*
Let's start with Best Buy for $2000.
Me: *That was my TVs for the new house.*
Jared: *Home Depot? $800?*
Me: *Dining room light.*
Jared: *Mattress Firm for $1200?*
Me: *Oh, the mattress for the guest room.*
Jared: *Leslie's Pools for $900?*
Me: *NO. Wait… yes, my Polaris.*
Jared: *Weirs Furniture for $3500?*
Me: *Um. My bedroom.*
Jared: *Blinds R Us for $2800?*
Me: *Okay. We can stop now.*
Jared: *Rug Outlet for $750?*
Me: *I said we can stop.*
Jared: *Ms. Bolt, I think we learned who stole your identity.*
Me: *Thank you.*

THE SECRET TO HAPPINESS IS LOW EXPECTATIONS

Smart ass.

Back to the move…

I had to give myself some grace. I'm in my early fifties and it is the first time I have ever lived alone. Never went away to college. Stayed with my folks, worked at the grocery store to pay for college, and commuted to the university in downtown Chicago on the subway. Never had an apartment. Got married out of the house I was born in.

I sat down in my four-bedroom, two-story house with a pool and wondered what I did to myself. Jeff was in his own house now. The kids were away in college. Less than an hour away, but still. For a person who craves certainty and security, this was terrifying. A complete reset. I was disoriented. There was a pit in my stomach, like when the power goes out in the middle of the night. *What was I thinking?*

I'll tell you what I wasn't thinking. That this was going to be one of the most significant years of my life, with several people and situations I never *expected* to enter stage right.

~ ~ ~ ~ ~

Sidebar: A year later Greg was driving Jeff somewhere. Jeff opened the center console in Greg's truck to get something and found a garage door opener.

Jeff: *Is this our garage door opener from the old house?*

Greg: *Yup.*

Jeff: *Why did you keep it?*

Greg: *Those people were such jerks to mom. I kept it to torture them.*

Jeff: *How?*

Greg: *Every time I drive by our old house, if the garage door is open, I close it. If it is closed, I open it. They're probably fighting about it all the time.*

That's my boy. ⋀

What's love got to do with it?

"Are we written in the stars? Or in the sand…?"
– Old Dominion

"Coincidence is God's way of remaining anonymous."
– Albert Einstein

What I learned the year after living-together-divorced and moving into that house is that it is never too late to get a reputation. I am a late bloomer. When other girls were trying on padded bras, I was playing with Barbies. I was thirty-five when I first inhaled. And sex? Twenty-three. And that's not the number of men. That's how old I was when I "did it". With Jeff. Yes, the one and only. We did not, however, wait until marriage, which was scandalous enough for me. The priest told me to say ten "Hail Mary's", six "Our Fathers", and one "Holy Cow".

So you can imagine my surprise when a month after I was on my own for the first time in my life in my fifties – I decided to fly across the country to spend a weekend with a veritable stranger.

Let me wrap some context around the events leading up to this. A couple years prior, Karen introduced me to one of her clients – a prominent plastic surgeon in Florida. He was upset with the profile a certain beauty magazine editor had written for him. *"Ask Isabel to rewrite it,"* she told him. He did and I did and in short order I was doing most of the surgeon's profiles in the magazine. I like to think I gave as many surgeons a "personality enhancement" as they gave women breast augmentations.

But I digress.

A bonus – some of them hired me to write marketing collateral for their practices. It was fun and a steady stream of extra income. It was also a challenge. When you think of the micro-detail plastic surgeons perform, you can imagine what is involved in their editing my work. One of them told me, *"We can pick fly shit out of pepper…"* Kept me on my toes and made me better. And occasionally furious. Like when they argued about comma placement for fifteen minutes. Or when they insisted I write, *"We treat our patients like family."* NO. And here's why. *"Do you know how most people treat their family?"* Plus the car dealership, hardware store, and pancake house already use that tagline with their customers. Stop it. Can we say something with more impact? Most ultimately complied. And now the rest of you know. *Don't say that.*

THE SECRET TO HAPPINESS IS LOW EXPECTATIONS

The previous August before my move, the phone rang. It was the beauty magazine. They wanted my permission to give a surgeon my phone number. I had written his profile, and he wanted to collaborate with me on some articles for his website and some journals. No, I didn't remember the name, but yes, I would be happy to work with him. His name was Aaron, and he ran a busy practice on the Upper East Side. I had been to New York a few times, but frankly, aside from seeing *Sex in the City*, I didn't know the real Manhattan from Boise. That was about to change.

We spoke on the phone about once a week. About his techniques related to fat transfer, tummy tucks, facial rejuvenation, and breast surgery. After about a month, he asked me not to call him "Doctor," call him Aaron. By Christmas I knew all about his three-year separation from his wife and his legal dilemmas. He had a young son. It was tearing him apart. I told him my story about living with my ex-husband. We discussed current events, politics, travel, and books. He was articulate, clever, and funny. And you know where this is going even though I didn't right away. I kept the conversations neutral.

In January…

Him: *Meet me at the convention in Las Vegas.*
Me: *Vegas is my idea of hell.*
Him: *Well, it's more about being together.*
Me: *No.*

My flirting was a bit rusty. Plus I was scared. So far, it was only five months of phone calls – like an Amish couple. I wasn't ready for a real man in person. But he was patient.

In March, he asked if I would come to visit him for the weekend. In a voice that didn't sound familiar, I said, *"Yes."* I attribute that to being in shock from my move the month before. Off balance, I lost my inner compass. Reality set in when I was in flight to New York having a panic attack. I remembered what Jean told me to do one time when I was freaked out about a presentation – *"Pretend you are someone else,"* she said. That helped. And it wasn't hard to do since I didn't know who I was anymore.

Aaron picked me up at LaGuardia. I got in his car. He must have sensed my fight or flight posture. Maybe my teeth were chattering.
Him: *Listen, we have lots of options. I can turn around and I'll get you a first class ticket home. Or we can drive outside the city and when we get to my house, you can pick one of my five bedrooms and stay there. Or we can sleep in my bed. It is completely up to you, Isabel.*
(So thoughtful. He disarmed me. Or he could be a serial killer.)
Me: Fine. *Just drive.*

We arrived. We had a cocktail and talked. He was cuter than his pictures. He said the same about me. He wasn't even close to what I considered "my type", but he had this *swagger*. I followed him upstairs. I cannot remember much after that. Except it was extraordinary. A gravitational pull that took my breath away. So *this* is what everyone talks about.

Afterward, I told him he was pretty good, but I didn't have a whole lot of comparison.

He got a kick out of that.

The affair had begun. Every third weekend or so, I would fly to New York, and we would have fun in the city or at his home outside Manhattan. Day trips or errands or writing for his practice. He gave me his car and his black AmEx card to do or buy what I wanted while he was in surgery. I met his staff and neighbors. Most importantly, this late bloomer was blooming. Once again, Keith Morrison was ringing in my ears from the latest *Dateline*. *It was a moment where biology worked its eternal magic...Then Barbara drove home, and Bill flew back to Montana — for weeks blissfully wrapped in a gauzy veil.* Something like that.

That first summer he surprised me with a long weekend in Nantucket. We flew on a six-seater plane and stayed at the Wauwinet--a famous old hotel with a lawn that sloped down into the sea. Our first evening was at the wharf. A platter of oysters and a martini were in front of me. The entire scene was a movie set. I grabbed Aaron's arm.

Me: *This is beyond anything I expected.*
Him: *I'm glad you like it.*
Me: *Thank you so much. I've never been to Maine before.*
Him: (long pause) *You're not in Maine.*
Me: *Where are we?*
Him: *Massachusetts. But I'll take you to Maine someday.*

In September, Aaron planned a special trip to Sea Island, Georgia – further down the East Coast, *"The opposite direction of Maine,"* he said. Very funny. We wined and dined and shot skeet and rode horses on the beach and… I found a lump. This wasn't possible. In July it was my five-year anniversary. I was cured. The doctors had been following me with special mammograms twice a year.

Aaron felt it. *"I don't think it's anything to worry about, but get it checked when you get home."*

Which is why he is a plastic surgeon and not an oncologist.

Another week of doctor visits and waiting to exhale. It was cancer. HOW?

They told me. *"We should have had you doing MRIs because of your dense tissue. And we should have probably had you see the oncologist more often. And maybe we shouldn't have discontinued the hormone therapy drug so soon…"*

I called Aaron, sobbing.

He was in the middle of a fight with his almost-ex-wife and son's teacher, and could he call me back later?

WHAT?

I heard a sound. It was the other shoe dropping. The one you wait for when things are going too well. There wasn't one doctor even pretending to take care of me. Including the one I was dating. I was on my own.

He called much later that day. But with a plan. I was to fire all the doctors in Texas, grab my records and fly to New York where he had doctors who were waiting for me. A breast cancer surgeon, an oncologist, a gynecologist, and him. They were, and are, a brilliant bunch.

The consensus was predictable but shocking. The best course of action was a double mastectomy. I heard "amputation". The people I had seen with mastectomies looked like they went three rounds with a shark. The scars and gashes and flaps. I went to bed for three days. I couldn't picture my body anymore. In my mind I never even thought about the cancer – only that I would be left looking like a Picasso.

Meantime, unbeknownst to me, Aaron was doing some research. The breast cancer surgeon he recommended for me was a colleague of his and the founder of a newish procedure at the time called a "skin and nipple sparing" mastectomy. Essentially, it involves keeping the patient's skin and nipples and just removing the tissue underneath and replacing it with silicone. The end result can potentially resemble a breast augmentation, but the cancer and all breast tissue are removed. This could be a prayer answered. But wait. Not every woman is a candidate including those who had prior radiation. Like me. Aaron tracked down a surgeon in Italy who often did the procedure on radiated breasts with no complications. Aaron was satisfied with the tips he got from him. He told me he could make it work. The surgery was scheduled for November 4th.

Most people getting a mastectomy go to a hospital for days depending upon the type of surgery. Bandages and pain meds and IVs. Aaron had his own certified operating suite in his office. I walked in, laid down, surrounded by his anesthesiologist, surgical tech, the famous breast cancer surgeon, and him. I woke up and walked to his recovery room across the hall where his nurse stayed with me that night. He flew my sister in, and we stayed in Aaron's apartment on the upper east side of Manhattan for the next night, then he drove us to his home where Joanna was with me for part of my recovery the first few days, then left. I stayed on his couch. I was tired, but no pain, a couple drains – that was IT. The great reveal was profound. I was…beautiful. Aaron did such an artist's job. As the stitches healed, I looked better than I ever would have *expected*. A miracle. Incredibly grateful to him. He took care of me after all.

I went back to Texas. We didn't see each other for a month or so because he was on his third lawyer, and he said he was not good company. This would be a recurring theme that escalated over time. Sometimes I would get to New York, and he would be silent for a day just dealing with lawyers and paperwork.

But then the sweetest moments would happen. The boy raised Jewish, taking me to St. Patrick's Cathedral for Christmas Mass. He and his son laying a rose petal path to the bathtub after I made Thanksgiving dinner for them at home. Stopping at an exclusive lingerie boutique to buy me something special after my operation so I would feel pretty. It was a La Perla piece that cost more than my wedding gown.

The next holiday season was getting a bit rocky between us, and we took a hiatus from one another. My family flew to San Diego for a college bowl game where David played linebacker. After getting settled into the hotel, Joanna took a shower. I heard a scream. Found her on the bathroom floor in terrible pain. It was her back. She could barely move. At first I didn't hear the phone ring. It was Aaron. How odd. Just when I didn't know what to do next. He talked Joanna off the bathroom floor and listened to her symptoms. He hung up. Called back a few minutes later. He found a pharmacy across the street from the hotel and had medication waiting for her. It would get her through the game, back home on the plane, and eventually into surgery.

Over four years, we had incredible long weekends in Amelia Island, Palmetto Bay, Boca Raton, and South Beach. He had a limousine waiting for me at the Schubert after a Broadway play and drivers hired for me to and from LaGuardia every weekend. We saw American Pharoah win the Triple Crown at the Belmont. We sat on a lawn for a benefit concert steps away from Tony Bennett. On New Years Eve we skied in Vermont. In the spring he arranged a trip to Berlin and Prague. But even when we stayed in, it was special for me. Just being together.

My attraction to him never waned. But by lawyer Number 6… his fanatical preoccupation with finding the right lawyer…
Me: *Put ME through law school. The way things are going, I will be able to represent you by the time I pass the bar.*

I realized with a sinking feeling that while I thought I was starring in *Love, Actually* – he was standing in for Michael Douglas in *War of the Roses*. His "ex" told him when he left her she would destroy him. She was. And eventually, she did.

In year four, by the time the driver dropped me off at LaGuardia, I couldn't recall the passion that seemed so real in the moment just hours before. Strange to share intimacy without any lasting affection. Walking on the beach, he was so preoccupied he wouldn't even hold my hand. Our weekends were like Chinese Food. Hungry a couple hours later. Like you hadn't eaten at all.

Thanksgiving was approaching. I was having a full house. Aaron mentioned he and his son had no plans and could they maybe come? I said no.

David: *Well, to me it looks like you've got twenty people coming and I don't remember any one of them saving your life.*

He was right. I told Aaron to come.

And this is where the story gets interesting.

The weekend before Thanksgiving, Gabby went into the hospital for a routine gallbladder surgery. In general, she is an educated health consumer. The exception is young handsome surgeons. She figured he knew the latest techniques. She had the surgery, went home the same day and planned to immediately rummage around her attic to bring more Christmas boxes down in prep for her annual holiday extravaganza. None of us would have blinked at this post op behavior. Pretty sure she's a descendant of Joan of Arc. Nothing stops her, except…Dr. Doolittle.

Within twelve hours, she is severely ill with abdominal pain. Like nothing she's had before. The next morning her daughter takes her in to see Dr. Doolittle. Gabby is crying and can barely walk. He presses on her tummy, and she screams. He tells her she is constipated. She is dismissed. Home that night, there is a fluorescent colored sticky liquid oozing out of her incisions. Pretty sure that is not a sign of constipation, Gabby wraps herself in a towel and *drives herself* to the ER. Tests are done. Her common bile duct had been severed. In case you failed anatomy, it is an essential part of your plumbing.

Thanksgiving was the next day, so Gabby had to wait until Saturday for a senior surgeon to reconstruct her biliary and intestinal tract. No one is saying anything about a mistake. They are calling it a "complication".

I was going to the hospital to be in the waiting room with her kids. Aaron wanted to come. He was suspicious. They weren't telling her everything. We got to the surgery floor. I went into the waiting room and…where was Aaron? *Oh no.* He went right through the "Prohibited" doors leading to the operating rooms. Told the staff he was a surgeon from New York and friend of the family and would like a word with Gabby's surgeon the minute it was convenient. Came back out and said, *"Just wanted them to know another surgeon would be asking some questions, so they better fix what they broke."* Indeed, the young surgeon came out.

His mentor, an older surgeon had done the reconstruction. He began drawing pictures for me and girls about how they did some sort of bypass. Aaron asked some questions. The other surgeon squirmed around, did some double talk, and left. And so did we. In the car Aaron said, *"The next couple days will be critical."* I saw Gabby later and she was sedated but aware.

December 1 – two days after the surgery – Gabby was living for the next dose of Dilaudid – a narcotic for extreme pain. This from a woman who only needs to bite a bullet for childbirth. I got a call from Jean who drove up from Houston to see her. She said Gabby told her she wants to die. Now I am panicking. Several doctors have been in and out of Gabby's room, all saying reassuring things, but all I can think of is they are planning to bury this mistake. I call Aaron, crying. We run through all the symptoms I've been able to get out of her. *"She is septic,"* he says. *"She has about twenty-four hours to turn this around."* NO, NO, NO! I was wailing. He said he would call me back with a plan and hung up. Two hours later the phone finally rang.

Aaron: *We're set. I called a colleague who is on the board of the University Medical Center. We went to medical school together. He is arranging for the head of liver transplant and critical biliary care to meet Gabby at the hospital. You have to get her transferred. He's waiting for her.*

I called Gabby, told her what Aaron said about her condition, and explained about the transfer. So ill, she hesitated, but I told her If she didn't take action in two hours, I would play my medical power of attorney card. She told the surgeon. The Dr.

THE SECRET TO HAPPINESS IS LOW EXPECTATIONS

Doolittle hospital takes fourteen hours to get her released – probably to scrub all the records. Gabby claims they threw her into a florist truck and deposited her at hospital #2. Better than a coroner's truck. Aaron's colleagues were waiting for her…just as promised. The brilliant specialist and his angel sidekick – an interventional radiologist – were eventually able to put Humpy Dumpty back together, but it was a long, long road to recovery.

Aaron and I were almost at the five-year mark. Lawyer #7 was hired. The tension was at a soul crushing decibel. Some would say long distance relationships are a challenge. For us, it was the distance when we were together. Despite some of the most memorable times of my life, Aaron's priorities were always the divorce, their son, his patients and then me. In that order. I had to admit, *I was a supporting actress in my own love story.* My heart was in a million pieces, and I had to say goodbye to another man. Again. To save myself. I thought God brought him into my life as a soulmate. In retrospect, that was not the case at all.

We didn't get to Maine. He never held my hand or told me he loved me. Once I left, I doubt if I ever crossed his mind.

But he got my sister home. He saved my best friend's life. He preserved my body image and femininity along with inspiring a serious dose of self-discovery. And I believe that's more than you can *expect* of a man who asked a magazine for a phone number.

Extremely Loud, Incredibly Close

*"Husbands come and go;
children come and eventually they go.
Friends grow up and move away.
But the one thing that's never lost is your sister."*
– Gail Sheehy

"If you didn't live here I would have to kick you out."
– Joanna (when I accidentally put away
dirty dishes from the washer)

The same year I moved into the big house and began commuting to NYC, another scud missile was about to land. My sister Joanna called. It was June. She was getting a divorce. Not a huge surprise and it wouldn't be too messy. No children, a house they built in Colorado would be split, and the only point of contention was custody of Cayman, their chihuahua-rat terrier mix. Knowing this wretched animal, I assumed neither wanted it. I was wrong. After much gnashing of teeth (the chihuahua's) she "won" full custody.

Back to the call. Joanna wanted to move to Dallas, and could she stay with me for three months or so until she got "on her feet"? I had plenty of room, so of course.

This July we will be celebrating our "14th anniversary" living together. Since she is five years younger than me, soon we will be under the same roof longer as adults than we were as children.

It started off a bit rocky because I was coerced into driving her thirteen hours from Colorado Springs to Dallas. I hate driving anywhere over two hours, much less with that creature in the front seat. I put my foot down on having my own hotel room the night before our expedition because she mentioned Cayman slept better with the TV on all night. *NO*. Joanna stayed in the animal friendly hotel, and I was across the street, getting points at the Hilton. In the morning we had to backtrack when we discovered we were going north. She mistakenly grabbed the map she used to get to Kansas City for a competition (more on that later.) Once we were going in the right direction, we decided we would rest once we got to Amarillo.

Joanna: *Armadillo would be a good place for lunch.*
Me: *You mean Amarillo. It means yellow in Spanish.*
Joanna: *No. Armadillo. I know my animals.*

Whatever. We made it to Dallas. She settled in. And it doesn't look like she'll be "on her feet" anytime soon.

THE SECRET TO HAPPINESS IS LOW EXPECTATIONS

Everyone would agree that you never know anyone until you live with them. In the case of Joanna, I never knew her too well, even when we were growing up. If you do the math, I was in college when she was in eighth grade – quite a gap. As adults, that gap closes considerably. Although we both have strong personalities, we are very different women, and that is why it all works. For the record, in our family tree, I am the empath and worrier. My mantra is: *"What if…?"*; Andrew is the family historian, creative genius, and bleeding heart passivist – a true middle child. His is *"They mean well"*; Joanna has a soft heart for all animals but can't tolerate most people in small or large doses. She is an activist against ignorance, laziness and stupidity, which keeps her quite busy. An example from the other day:
Joanna: *You know how people say, "Choose your battles"?*
Me: *Yes.*
Joanna: *Well, I don't. I want to do every single one.*
There is never any confusion about where she stands.

She immediately set about decorating her bedroom. Mermaid sheets, a whale sculpture, dolphin pictures, seashells, and an original painting of that dog. The man cleaning the carpets asked me how old my daughter was. I lied and said twelve. Ordinarily, I keep the door closed.

At the time, Joanna had thirty years under her belt as a nurse. Her career began in a hospital in downtown Chicago. After college, Andrew moved to Los Angeles for work, and Joanna joined him a few years later. She worked in L.A. at the hospital

NICU, the OR, and finally in a famous plastic surgeon's office in Beverly Hills.

> **Sidebar:** In a twist of fate, *I met Karen through Joanna*. A chance meeting that would eventually impact my life in the most *unexpected* ways. Karen was doing a practice management consultation with the surgeon Joanna worked with. While interviewing Joanna, Karen mentioned she was looking for a writer.
> Joanna: *My sister is a writer in Dallas.*
> She based this on the fact that I did some editing for a doctor she once worked for and corrected her book reports in high school. Okay, I wrote them. And the few times when I authored letters when she wanted to tell someone off.
> Joanna: *Start with "To whom it may concern:" Then take it from there.*
>
> She calls to tell me to expect a call from Karen, who I learn is the founder and president of a sixty-person consulting firm on Michigan Avenue in Chicago.
> Me: *What is wrong with you? I am not a writer. I sell contract furniture.*
> Joanna: *Do you write for people?*
> Me: *Sometimes, but...*
> Joanna: *Do you still live in Dallas?*
> Me: *Yes*
> Joanna: *Then you are a writer in Dallas. Shut up.*
> My sister, the literary agent.

THE SECRET TO HAPPINESS IS LOW EXPECTATIONS

Back to nursing. With her credentials, she had zero trouble landing a job at the university medical center. It was in the clinic for people with head and neck cancers and she was assigned to the busiest surgeon. The one everyone was afraid of. Demanding, dedicated, impatient with bureaucracy and a perfectionist. Since he was her mirror image, it wasn't long before she was the yin to his yang. It is grueling work, physically, mentally, and emotionally. Joanna is present at all the consultations. She sees the patients before and after surgery, and in between she is educating them and their caregivers. Tracheotomies, jaws and tongues being removed, neck flaps…conditions generally affect breathing, speaking, or swallowing, so there is a level of urgency only trumped by the sheer complexity of arranging treatment and recovery.

Joanna loves her doctor. She told me once he is so devoted to his calling, she feels like she works for Jesus. What puts her over the edge is the combination of his workload, staffing shortages (including people who are there, just not working), patients who are apathetic about following treatment protocol, patients who let something grow for years and now want surgery next Tuesday, and the devils at insurance companies who don't think head and neck cancer surgery is all that necessary. It's beyond maddening.

Which is why at the end of one clinic day, she brought the "to do" folder to her doctor, opened it up and on the top page was a post it note where she had written "Fuck."
Doctor: *What's that about?*

Joanna: *Annette* (her supervisor) *won't let me say it out loud anymore. So I have to write it.*
There were dozens more "fucks" inside the pages. She is always out of Post-it notes.

Soon after moving in and getting her job, it was time to find a boyfriend. She went online and after suffering through a handful of jokers, she snags Scott. Perfect for her in every way except he is not much of an animal lover. That was about to change. Cayman and Joanna were a package deal. He relented with the stipulation that I have custody every other weekend.

Joanna is fierce and determined but inside there is a chewy center. If she were candy, it would look like a jawbreaker on the outside and a marshmallow fluff inside. It goes well beyond the workday. And I mean the jawbreaker part.

Joanna has a history of choosing a hobby and attacking it, not so much as a pastime, but more like something you'd see in a crusader. In her younger days it was gymnastics, then marathons, and on to martial arts. Her honeymoon was climbing Kilimanjaro.
Me: *You are a "fanatic".*
Joanna: *A fanatic is what lazy people call those of us with goals.*

Now I have a front row seat for all her obsessions.
Joanna's boxes were all checked: move, job, boyfriend…and now she is searching for her next "hobby". There she goes –

THE SECRET TO HAPPINESS IS LOW EXPECTATIONS

heading out the door after work in tights. To ballet class. She is fifty-six. No one told her.

Ballet soon swallowed her whole. Books, lessons, movies, documentaries, music. David says her immersion makes Tom Brady look like he skims the playbook. What began as an innocent interest in ballet turned into five days a week of lessons and videos and *Swan Lake* wafting through the house at all hours. I don't say much. I did laugh at some of the wardrobe malfunctions.
Joanna: *Damn it. I think I just sewed my pants to my toe shoe ribbons. Ballerinas do this in between performances.*
And the shrug she got for her birthday from the boys? She tried it on and almost tied her hands behind her back.

She is still dating Scott who should be canonized. He sees her at his place one night overnight a week because her dance and her dreadful dog come first. He knows he is in third place. I don't get it. Dog got sprayed by a skunk in his yard last week. It wasn't "my weekend", so this time she took that horrid pet with her. I asked Scott how long it took him to train that skunk. Of course, smelly dog wound up in my house post vet treatment at 1:00 a.m. House smelled like burning rubber for days.

The obsession grew and soon we were attending recitals.*
Me to Scott: *Was the last girl on* Match *really all that bad?*
Scott: *I'm no quitter.*
No, he is not.

> **Sidebar:** *Adding insult to injury, Joanna was listed in the program as Preama Bolt. No getting over that. Especially considering my sister's lifelong battle to get others to pronounce and spell her name correctly. It is J-O-A-N-N-A. Reasonably simple. Apparently not. A steady stream of Joanne, Johanna, Jonnana…once at Starbucks her cup came back with JoeAne written on it. There was an altercation. Similar to the one at Ulta when the cashier would not accept her coupons and the manager had to be called because Joanna told them Ulta was "F**Ked Up." She was escorted out. She really needs to keep Post-Its in her purse.

Aside from recitals, Joanna also ropes Scott into field trips like goat yoga. I went along. You get to pet dirty farm animals while you do yoga poses. The place was packed. They also had a pot belly pig running around. Despite the dozen goats, everyone wanted the pig. Except he wouldn't leave Scott's side. As usual, the universe acts out with reverse attraction. What you are most repelled by becomes a magnet. Poor Scott is also the proud owner of a stray cat Joanna made him adopt. One thousand dollars in vet bills later, "Chester" has the run of the house. Joanna also asked him to adopt a penguin at the zoo. That was only $100, but you don't bring them home.

Back to ballet – at the four-year mark, she was still going strong. Kind of. Despite her knee, calf, back and neck injuries. Patches, hot pads, and visits to the chiropractor. Reminds me of that comic Brian Regan. He puts his hand on the front of his upper thigh and says, *"Doctor this is the only part of me that doesn't hurt. Can you make the rest of me feel like this?"*

Theoretically, she should be part of the New York City ballet corps by now.

Do you remember *The Dating Game*? Did you know there is now a Celebrity version? We didn't either. It came on accidentally.
Me: *Joanna get in here, it's the* Dating Game *hosted by some twit and Michael Bolton. Michael Bolton!*
Joanna: *He looks terrible. I hope he's not going to sing.*
Me: *Look at him. Oh no, he's starting to sing.*
Joanna: *Only his lips are moving. He looks exactly like me after ballet.*

~ ~ ~ ~ ~

Never mind *The Dating Game*. *Dateline* is our drug. Joanna and I love Keith Morrison. We call him "The Skeleton Man". We are soothed by his voice. *"And soon, poison and anxiety seeped under Jason's door and through his windows and into his nerve endings and he wondered why they were late…"*

I'm not sure if he writes the things he says, but he is a riot.

We've seen all the episodes of *Dateline*, but we don't remember any of the endings, so it's like *Groundhog Day*. When we get to the end, we look at each other and say, *"We've SEEN THIS ONE."* We are disgusted.

We alternate with *Perry Mason*. We love it when District Attorney Hamilton Burger and Perry get into it.

Burger: *Your honor, I object. Argumentative. Mr. Mason, once again, is assuming a fact not in evidence. These "leading" questions are incompetent, irrelevant, and immaterial. They deal with matters not covered in direct examination.*

Poor Burger. Never won a case.

Then there is *The Bachelor*.

Me: *Isn't it nice they give the couples a chance to talk all night and get to know each other without cameras in the fantasy suite?*

Joanna: *You are such a dork. They are having SEX.*

Me: *You are kidding.*

Joanna: *At this point I have decided to stop making fun of you and start taking care of you.*

Back to *Dateline* – it is not only entertaining, but also my barometer on relationships. Last week a woman killed her husband with rat poison. Her new fiancé says he is with her because, "*She is everything a man looks for in a woman.*"

Then there is the woman, married with seven children, in the process of divorcing her husband while dating his best friend. She recruits her two oldest sons to ambush the husband in his townhome basement. The three of them strangle, stab, and bludgeon him to death.

Time goes by. Best friend (now fiancé) and woman move in together and later decide to move to another state. Detectives finally find enough evidence to charge everyone with murder except the boyfriend.

Dateline host to boyfriend: *Do you think you'll ever find love again?*

Fiancé: *I don't think so. She set the bar pretty high.*

Finally, Ernie III is a poker player and a player in general. Has a wife and son at home but four different girlfriends in different cities. His parents, Ernie Junior, and mother have been brutally murdered. One night in New Orleans, he meets a woman online and takes her to dinner. Explains his parents have been murdered. Oh. And he is writing a novel about murdering parents. Hmmm. He asks her to his hotel room. She goes. She notices bungee cords everywhere. Why? Well, in case he has to escape from people searching for him by jumping off the balcony. She spends the night with him anyway.

Joanna: *You don't have a chance.*

~ ~ ~ ~ ~

Despite her cutting commentary, overall, Joanna is pretty low maintenance. She is OCD about "her shelf in the refrigerator" and keeps dozens of Tupperware and plastic water containers in my cabinets. She acts like it is a mortal sin to intermingle our laundry. When Greg lived with us during summers in college, she had him put four hooks in her bathroom. She uses a certain towel for each part of her body. One night he told her he switched them around when she was at work. She had convulsions. We laughed. That was mean.

She got me back on her sixtieth birthday and it wasn't even her fault. It was happening the same spring as David and Kristen's wedding. Her birthday in April, the wedding in May. I was planning on getting her the whale tail necklace, the Baryshnikov book, and tights she wanted. That would be that. However. It was February when Kristen, my now daughter-in-law innocently turned everyone's world upside down. By "everyone" I mean Gabby. And by "world" I mean the wedding shower. Let me explain.

From the moment David gave Kristen a ring, Gabby has been gathering props in advance of Kristen's wedding shower. Truth is, Gabby has been collecting ideas since the boys were in high school just in case they got someone pregnant, so she would never be caught unprepared to launch the extravaganza. In fact, I'm sure she was secretly hoping for a shotgun wedding so she could do a wedding shower and a baby shower in the same year. She *lives* for showers. And celebrations of any kind.

One evening, the kids were over, and I asked Kristen to give me a couple dates that suited her schedule. She had a strange reaction. Mentioned something about her mother doing a shower in April and changed the subject. The next day David calls.

David: *Mom, we have to have a serious conversation.*
Me: *Is it about one of those characters you picked for groomsmen?*
David: *No, it's Kristen. She doesn't want a shower from our side.*
Me: *I don't understand your broken English. Every bride gets a shower from the groom's side.*

THE SECRET TO HAPPINESS IS LOW EXPECTATIONS

David: *No. And please don't push her. She says she would be uncomfortable because she won't know anyone.*

I admit that stopped me in my tracks. I didn't know much about being a mother-in-law, but reasonably sure fighting with my future daughter-in-law about a shower would not be a good start.
I had to let it go.
And find a way to sedate Gabby before telling her. So many things just roll off her back, but throw a fire wall up between her and a party? *No sir.* She did not take it well. Had already bought the miniature chicks wearing bridal veils for each place setting.

Joanna was within earshot during my tenth conversation with Gabby about why we couldn't have a shower.
Joanna: *I'm going to have my sixtieth birthday in a couple months. Why don't you leave Kristen alone and give me a party?*
Gabby's head spun around like the exorcist. *Why not? An epic sixtieth party.* She was back in the saddle.

And that is when the gates of hell opened.

Here was our first discussion:
Me: *Before you get too wound up, I am paying for everything. You provide the house, and we can talk about themes and ideas, but first I need to give you a budget.*
Gabby: *Aren't you putting the cart before the horse?*

She thought the horse was the party planner and the cart just filled up with money along the way.

It was going to be a ballerina and animal theme in honor of my sister's obsessions and decorated in her favorite color: periwinkle. You know, the kind of party most eight-year-old's dream about. Gabby and I each had our list of things to do, but that did not stop her from calling me three times a day checking on where I was on my list. Did I get the photos copied? What about the frame sizes? Where was the easel? How were we doing on the mock photo booth? Were twelve dozen cookies in the shapes of dolphins, dog bones, and piglets enough for thirty-two people? Should we serve lavender tea to match the color theme? Did I order the life-size cutout of a ballerina? What color should the balloons be? How many votives? When can I bring over the ballet slippers? For god's sake, *it was still six weeks till the party.* Gabby casually mentioned the idea of replacing the flowers in front of her house with a color to match the party theme. I explained the budget did not include landscaping. She was driving me insane. In retrospect, I would have rather had the IRS after me.

But what a party it was. My favorite part was the surprises. Joanna knew about the party and gave us the guest list, but I added in some of her best friends from out of town without telling her. Theresa from Iowa, our cousin Vicki from Chicago, and her two best friends from elementary school – Terry and Peggy. It was a tactical triumph sneaking everyone into town. Terry and Peggy surprised her at the hospital in an exam room

THE SECRET TO HAPPINESS IS LOW EXPECTATIONS

posing as patients. And Theresa and Vicki were hiding in the house when she returned with the other girls. It was good to see someone accustomed to being in charge, so off balance. The party was a riot and such a success – family, friends, coworkers. Joanna was so excited.

Post-party, her only critique was that it would have been nice to have a petting zoo…I have no words. But Scott did. He took her to Fredericksburg, Texas, where you can wash elephants. In case you were wondering where one does that, now you know. She came home with a canvas of an elephant footprint and hung it in her bedroom next to the ballerina artwork and the shadow box with her toe shoes.

Yes, after her party and elephant bathing, she hung up her toe shoes for good. Her knees, ankles, neck, ribs – anyway she was running out of joints, and she still couldn't understand French after four years, going five times per week, so it was time for a new obsession.

Also, after the party, just when I thought the coast was clear (and the elephants weren't even dry)…the phone rings. Gabby wants to know *if I can ask Greg when he is proposing to Jodi* because then she will know the season she can get the house ready for Jodi's shower. If Greg knew about this conversation he would have had a seizure. In case you are not paying attention, I seem to be surrounded by fanatics.

Meantime, for my birthday, the kids bought me a golf lesson. I think to teach me how to retire since I suck at it. Now that her ballet career was over, Joanna had some free time. We signed up with Mackay Flanagan. It's funny how some people's names dictate their career. What else could he be but a golfer? Anyway, I am taking lessons. Joanna, on the other hand, is training for the LPGA tour. She bought a net for the backyard and runs to the simulator after work. I get home and the golf channel is on. During one of her lessons, Mackay made the fatal error of mentioning she might want to do the same thing with her wrist as I do. I don't know what I do with my wrist…but now to Joanna, it is GAME ON. I'm secretly scared of her. Scott is delighted. Not only does he love golf, but now they can play together. Plus, no dogs are allowed on the courses.

It took about a month, and although she was beating golf into submission, she decided she would also embark on something she is calling a "transformation". When Joanna first moved in, she had just wrapped up several years in Colorado doing physique body building – even earning a pro card. This is why we almost wound up in Kansas City – the location of her final competition. It's a body building pursuit where you wear a bikini and high heels and spray tan and walk around the stage posing. Incidentally, the bikini can fit in a shot glass. Obviously competitors are in tip top shape. Usually in their twenties. Joanna competed in the "masters" division in her late forties. I don't know what they call it when you are in your sixties…but we are about to find out.

I was still recovering from being tortured for years in her quest to become a prima ballerina at the age of sixty. Replace "ballet" with "body building" and you get the picture. She is up at 3:00 a.m. every day. Goes to the gym from 4:00 to 6:30 every morning. Then, gets ready for work. There is a scale in my kitchen where she weighs all her food. The blender never stops. Motivational podcasts ring in her ear buds. Counts macros and protein and ketones. Takes a roller bag with food in it to work so she can eat every ninety minutes. The Amazon truck backs into our driveway on a regular basis with cartons of vitamins.

She has a coach in Las Vegas who tracks her weekly progress. Before a competition, she gets a posing coach that shows her how to turn around on stage wearing five-inch heels and two strings. Such singular focus is simply incredible to watch. So driven. Last year she came in fifth overall (impressive) in the sixty and older division in a Pittsburgh show. There were twenty-one competitors in that range. Over sixty. Running around naked on a stage. The whole thing is startling to say the least.

Footnote: This year Joanna placed #1 in a national show, earning her Pro Card. Now, there will be no stopping her.

I watch from the couch drinking my wine. I go to the gym, occasionally wear a bikini, and do get a spray tan now and then, but that is where the similarities stop. She is quite an inspiration. I don't miss the track of *The Nutcracker* coming from her room for hours. So, there's that consolation.

The only time we don't get along is when the subject is food. It is irritating as hell when she won't eat anything I make that has butter, spices, marinade, sauce, olive oil, or taste. She'll whip out her oatmeal egg white protein powder bricks and cover them with calorie free syrup. I bought her ground chicken that was 96% fat free. She gave it back. Needs 98% fat free. The other day she weighed her ground chicken for lunch. Not enough protein. So she added tuna. Mixed it with the chicken and covered it in mustard and soy sauce. The next night I made a beautiful, herbed turkey breast. She nibbled at it. *"It has a bad aftertaste,"* she said.

Scott is hanging on. They get together in whatever time she has left between nursing, her dog, and the gym. I guess it works for them. David: *"They are each other's one size fits one."* The other day she posted on Instagram: *"When I first met you, I never knew how much you would someday mean to me…"* For Scott? NO. The picture above the text was a thirty-pound weight at the gym. A love letter to a piece of gym equipment.

If you are wondering, all this coaching and gym fees and vitamins are expensive. In September, Joanna announced she needed to "manifest" $15K by April. Evidently, it costs a lot to be her. She was almost finished with her vision board when her nurse friend at work had an idea. Said someone she knows makes a ton of money selling her feet online. The next thing I know Joanna comes home with three shopping bags full of props and half my sandals are missing. Pause for a moment to

THE SECRET TO HAPPINESS IS LOW EXPECTATIONS

let that sink in. My sister is posting photographs for men with foot fetishes.

Greg: *Foot porn? Oh, yeah. That is popular with weirdos.*
David: *I consider myself to have a wild imagination. That never would have occurred to me.*
Me: *For god's sake, don't breathe a word of this to Scott.*
Turns out he was already taking pictures for her to post. Said he knows what guys like.

Oh. Never mind.

Another money-making opportunity appeared at work. It was a new incentive for nurses called a "Clinical Ladder". You do a bunch of things on a list to be a better nurse and leader and create a booklet. The scoring would be one through four. If you get a four, you "win" $8K and some kind of distinction. She was hooked. Joanna will run through brick walls for a trophy of any kind. Incidentally, under the team building tab, Joanna arranged a Christmas party activity for all the nurses. I mentioned a carriage ride through Highland Park to see the lights. She chose axe throwing. Not sure how that fits into holiday spirit, but it gives you a glimpse into the personality I deal with.

Living with her on this ladder for months was getting on my last nerve. Finally, it was finished. HR and some Faculty graded it. She got a two. *Oh no. Oh no.* The brick wall won. She called a meeting with the judge and jury and brought the house down. Gave them the Gettysburg Address on nurse mistreatment and demotivation especially since the year of COVID. They relented and begrudgingly gave her a three. Off she went to tell all her nurses and medical assistants in her pod to never waste their time on this ladder. Scorched earth policy.

I was particularly impressed with her speech.
Isabel: *You should give the convocation speech at a nursing college graduation.*
Joanna: *I would have to start by apologizing that I'm four years too late to warn them.*

The jawbreaker. All full of bravado.

~ ~ ~ ~ ~

But last Friday I saw her when she came home late from work. Red-rimmed eyes. Her phone rang after hours in the clinic. It was a man who was her patient for years. He was calling from the hospital. The doctors were releasing him. Everything had metastasized. It was time to go home to hospice and he might have only a couple weeks. Wanted to tell her before it was too late how much her care, concern, and words of encouragement had meant to him and his family. Did she know she made all the difference? How she was always there when he needed her? That he loved her. And wished her a beautiful life.

And so do I. ⌂

Rations & Rants

"Any pot is no-stick if you no cook in it. Get cooking."
– Hallmark Card

I bought a Groupon for a write-your-own cookbook. It was supposed to be a Christmas gift for Gabby, but she was too busy dragging a twelve-foot tree into her living room, buying 400 yards of ribbon, and climbing into her attic to get the forty-seven snow villages down. I couldn't let the $20 I just spent go to waste, so I decided to use it for myself. Thought I would give it to the boys as a keepsake since at the time, they were both dating girls who struggled with crackers and cheese. You've heard the saying, *"She couldn't boil water"*? I was in the lake house kitchen when a teenaged blonde thing asked if she could help. I said when the water boils, put the beans in the pot. She wanted to know how she could tell. Not only couldn't boil water, she couldn't tell when…But never mind.

I titled my cookbook after the restaurant Greg said he would one day buy me. He calls it *Rations & Rants*. When I'm in my kitchen, I usually share my opinions on a variety of topics with anyone within earshot: People wearing masks in their cars – alone, why some folks wake up every day looking for something to be offended by, vegan diets, people who don't write thank you notes, how no one seems to dress properly anymore – I could go on and on. And I do. That's why *Rations & Rants* is so brilliant.

Greg pictures a chalkboard outside the restaurant with the Rant-of-the-Day, so people could decide if they were interested in my topic along with something to eat. In other words, no one will be served until they hear my point of view. In the vast majority of cases, my cooking is not nearly as good as my friend Jean's, but better than most. If you are hungry, it is well worth listening to the rant, even if you disagree with me. As Madonna once said, *"Everyone is entitled to my opinion."*

Choosing the recipes for the book was no small task since I have as many recipe books as Gabby has snow villages. My favorites are stuffed in a broken black binder, mostly handwritten on scraps of paper. It was a trip down memory lane. Grandma's strudel, my mom's beef rouladen, lake house birthday cake, Sue Ellen's chicken and biscuits, Twiddle's beer bread, Jean's beef tenderloin, Mrs. Comerford's egg casserole, Aunty Terry's Christmas nuts. Feeding people is therapy for me. It's intimate. Expressive. It reminds me of gatherings and occasions I'll never take for granted. When the high school varsity

THE SECRET TO HAPPINESS IS LOW EXPECTATIONS

defense piled into my kitchen on Wednesdays, ordering from Jimmy John's would not have been the same as seeing them in a feeding frenzy over pans of lasagna.

The template for the book began with having the "author" fill out their "rules of the kitchen". The perfect rant warm-up. Here are a few of my thinly veiled "rants" about the "rules":

- The better the ingredients, the better the outcome. This is a metaphor for life. No amount of sauce is going to cover up a bad piece of meat.
- Microwave cooking is an oxymoron. You can heat it or melt it – but that's it. Microwaved stuffed peppers can't touch Gramma's stuffed peppers simmering all day on the stove. Remember the microwave "Angry Chicken" recipe? *"You put a chicken in the microwave and it's going to get angry."* Case closed.
- Organic is a hoax.
- You can use fat free milk, fat free sour cream, fat free soup, fat free butter, then tell me what it tastes like. Notebook paper.
- Always double the garlic.
- There is a difference between cooking sherry and sherry for cooking. The former tastes like acid. Go to the liquor store.
- The meat closest to the bone is the most tender. So is the person across the table from you. Put down your phone and have a conversation.

- Don't let anything sit out for more than two hours or it will get "funny".
- Every soup, sauce, or stew is always better the second day.
- Notice I didn't include a lot of appetizers or salads. Buy those. No one ever remembers a cheeseball. Focus on the main dish. Another metaphor.

The beauty of the book's format was posting the recipe, then a personal note about it. Where you got it, what you served it with, tips, tricks, and so on.

Sweet and Sour Meatballs –
Note: Some people buy the frozen Italian meatballs and just throw those in the slow cooker. It saves time but it tastes like rubber. You decide.

Slow cooker tortilla soup –
Note: This recipe is so easy. Don't put bagged corn chips on top. Aren't you ashamed you can't even cut up and fry a tortilla?

The family-from-Italy-not-to-be-named Pasta Sauce –
Note: This is a sauce handed down generations from my friend who married their son. I saw *The Godfather*, hence, not naming names. The best thing she got out of the marriage was this sauce. It is remarkable. May she rest in peace.*
*She died of Leukemia and Lymphoma and a broken heart. Her husband on the day of the funeral: *"You think cancer is bad?*

THE SECRET TO HAPPINESS IS LOW EXPECTATIONS

Try taking care of someone with it." Which he never did anyway. He didn't deserve her. But she never let that spill into her kitchen.

Lisa's Baked Brisket –
Note: The best ever. Delicious. But slice against the grain or you can't chew it. Greg is a master at meat cutting. Greg is also mentioned under Corned Beef, Pot Roast and…

Roast turkey –
Notes:

- First of all, a turkey is just a big chicken, so I don't know why it is such a mystery and fuss for people.
- You will hear lots of noise about the dangers of putting stuffing in the bird. This is nonsense.
- Stop cooking a turkey for six hours unless it is forty pounds. You will be eating dust.
- Important: Do not let amateurs cut the finished bird. Greg does a surgeon's job. We have been witnesses to Thanksgivings where people use an ax. Makes it unappetizing and Greg gets a migraine watching.

Stuffing –
Note: My homemade stuffing has always been a hit. But there is a caveat. Apart from all the FRESH ingredients listed, you will see two boxes of Stove Top dressing. NEVER, NEVER, NEVER tell anyone this. Do what I do. Take the empty Stove Top boxes and wrap them in a bag and put them in another

bag and drop them in someone else's trash in the alley before anyone comes over.

Filet Mignon with Merlot –
Note: Use a meat thermometer.
145 degrees=medium rare
160 degrees=medium
170 degrees=someone who doesn't deserve steak. Give them spaghetti in a can.

Hash Brown Casserole –
Notes: This recipe is famous, not only because it is good, but because Aunty Gabby and I could never find a copy when we needed it. One of us always lost it and would have to call the other and say, *"I don't know how to tell you this, but I cannot find a copy of that damn potato casserole."* When I was looking for the recipe for my cookbook, I found a stack of twelve copies in back of the binder.

Jean's Beef Tenderloin –
I used to be sick buying a $120 piece of meat and praying it wouldn't be overcooked. But Jean gave me the secret. Along with the horseradish sauce…perfect every time. Made it for David's birthday and packed up the leftovers along with a jar of sauce on the side.
The next day:
David: *Thanks for the dinner, Mom.*
Me: *How are the leftovers? Isn't that sauce out of this world?*
David: *Oh, yeah.*

Later that day I find the beef gone but sauce still in my fridge. He forgot to take it. I called him back.

Me: *You never took the sauce. Makes me wonder what else you've lied to me about.*

David: *All of high school. All of college.*

Guess I should be grateful.

Carrie's Crack pudding –
Note: during a Grape Girls' weekend at the lake house, we all bumped into each other armed with spoons after midnight eating it right out of the refrigerator.

Greg is saving up for my restaurant. Meanwhile if you happen to come by around dinnertime, you will be served a portion of these rants alongside something delicious.

Warning: Controversial opinions ahead. Keep in mind, this is MY kitchen.

THE RANTS

- Names of children. We were at church one baptism Sunday. The names were Jet, Prince, Raine, and a girl named Chestlie. The boys said it sounded like horses at the track. When I am queen, this will change, because I will be naming all the children. There will be no Paris, London, or Zealand. No spelling contests like Laurie, Lori, Loree, or Laurey. No boys given dog names like Angus or girls named Heaven. And few Courtneys.

When David was in fourth grade there were fifteen of them.
- Road rage – Although the evidence is ubiquitous, no one will ever admit to being a bad driver.

  Rules of the road you might have missed when you got your license…if I let you merge in front of me, WAVE. If you are in the left lane to turn on a green light, PULL UP. All the way up so more than just you can get through on the yellow. If you have a handicapped sticker, don't drive with the sticker hanging on your rear view mirror. You are compounding the situation by cutting your line of sight. The sticker states to *only display it after you park*. And if an ambulance is behind you, PULL OVER AND STOP. Then make the sign of the cross. I don't care what religion you are. And FYI, Volvos are not inherently safe – it's the type of people that buy those cars. Never seen one go over fifty mph. And if you drive a PT Cruiser, rest assured we have nothing in common.
- Children on airplanes – Two words. Medicate them.
- Attire: if you are over forty – even if you are at your high school weight and definitely if you are not, it's time to stop shopping at Forever 21.
- Don't bring your coffee into a traditional church service. The sanctuary is not Starbucks.
- Paxlovid. You were a good citizen and got Pfizer's COVID-19 vaccine and booster so you wouldn't get the virus. You got sick anyway? Don't worry, there is an oral treatment to lessen your symptoms and pre-

vent hospitalization. It's called Paxlovid. A medicine to take when the first medicine didn't work. Also by Pfizer. *Hmmm.*

- And speaking of drugs, why is it on drug ads that all the side effects are part of why you are taking them in the first place? Migraine meds that give you headaches? Anti-osteoporosis medication that can cause hip and thigh fractures? Anti-depressants that make you want to kill yourself?

Lately I have been getting *People* magazine delivered every week. I don't recall subscribing. Probably pressed some button. Anyway, it is a treasure trove of prospective rants. We are in the twilight zone. I don't know even a few of the people in *People*. Taylor Swift maybe. The rest are competing for the "height of irrelevance" or perhaps shock value. Is it true that the rich and famous are having babies with their boyfriends, but only gay people are getting married? FYI—a pregnant Cardi B reunited with husband, Offset, to celebrate son, Wave's airplane themed third birthday amid their divorce. (I don't know whether to be more upset about her pregnant-by-whom?-yet-not-divorced-status, or their names.) And here is another cover with Drew Barrymore. ET was in 1982. Can everyone agree we are over her? Ryan Seacrest is taking over *Wheel of Fortune* aside from his other three host roles. Just like Michael Strahan and Rob Lowe. All of them must have body doubles. Are there only a dozen people going around the bathtub of Hollywood? And did I just see that Survivor was given another season? Who watches that?

Then there's the 2023 Grammys – the first non-binary and trans couple to get a Grammy for their song "Unholy." That indicates at least a bit of self-awareness. And I'm watching TV last week and a drug ad comes on and warns: *If you identified as a female at birth, don't take this drug.*

It's official. Jesus is coming back soon.

The beauty of rants is there will always be plenty of material. Fortunately, between cancel culture and "wokeness" there exists an unending stream of lunacy with nowhere to hide.

CNN tells us that the Disinformation Panel was shut down because of "disinformation that came from outside forces…" Other news programs celebrated for investigative reporting are now under investigation. The insanity is pervasive.

Then there is this: *Caitlyn Jenner claimed that O.J. Simpson once told his ex-wife Nicole Brown that he would one day «kill her and get away with it.» The allegation was made during "her" appearance on "Big Brother VIP" in Australia. The 72-year-old, who was once married to Brown's best friend Kris Jenner, spoke out about how the case impacted "her" family.*

I cannot follow the pronouns fast enough.

Speaking of the Kardashians, have you heard that Kim has declared this year "the year she will stop focusing on others so much and do more self-care?" Good to know.

THE SECRET TO HAPPINESS IS LOW EXPECTATIONS

The shocking, misguided direction of corporations and their virtue signaling gives me a headache. It is on brilliant display at one of the most highly reputed consulting companies in the world, where my son happens to work. It is frustrating for Greg, but a source of constant entertainment for me, David and Joanna. As a consultant, Greg has a front row seat to the HR department's "woke" corporate wisdom announced on email almost daily. A seemingly infinite capacity for embarrassment. Here is an example:

Greg texts *a screen shot from HR* for Pride Month (which followed closely behind Equity month, Social Justice month and People of Color month.) A long email about the celebrations including something about meeting at Apollo, and how important sensitivity is and how *everyone will hereby immediately be required to change their email signatures.*

Greg: *We are picking pronouns today.*

Me: *Ask they/them when white privilege month is. I'll be in the kitchen waiting for a reaction.*

Joanna: *I am offended by the name Apollo. "He/Him" was a "Greek" god. My pronouns are "never" and "nobody."*

David: *My pronouns are "none" and "whatsoever." I've left a picture of my lower half in all of your emails. Please check spam.*

Meanwhile, *Time* magazine's "Man of the Year" is actually a woman. The armed forces are making maternity wear for fighter pilots. The border is wide open, and here's a surprise: 100,000 people died of Fentanyl poisoning last year. Iran and Afghanistan have all our weapons and Ukraine has all our money. China is licking their chops. Inflation is at a forty-year high. Men are competing in women's sports and doing quite well, it turns out. The opening ceremonies at the Paris Olympics featured a Last Supper parody in drag. Crime is rampant. Parents are buying their children AK-47s for Christmas. Cities are swarming with homeless encampments. The media's propaganda is tearing the USA apart. We are on the brink of disaster on every conceivable front.

Just in case you are wondering when the people will wake up and the revolution will begin, have no fear – there is outrage. Here is what was on my feed last week –
News Headline: *Kellogg's sued $5M for not putting enough strawberry filling in their pop tarts.*
Bastards.

Dinner's ready. ⋀

Flats are for Quitters

"Everything goes with a perky bootie."
— Fitness Instructor at Equinox

"Why don't you turn your magic all the way the fuck on?"
— Jade, on *Instagram*

Earlier in the year, I had foot surgery to put an implant in a hole in my toe joint. According to the surgeon, we were lucky to discover this so she could solve my future foot problems. It was found on an MRI when I broke my foot in two places by falling off my high heels the previous November. Completely sober I might add. Tripped off a curb while carrying presentation booklets into the showroom. *"We are women who lug too much,"* Gabby often said. Anyway, the "fix" cost over $14K for an implant a quarter the size of a piece of corn. This is roughly twice what I paid for my other implants placed a bit higher. But I digress. So, I start the year in a boot which incidentally I covered in rhinestones.

After five months of hobbling around, the foot wasn't healing. Surgeon said, *"This never happens."* In the same tone of voice I hear every time I call the corporate help desk for computer problems. *"This never happens."* At which time they "escalate" my issue.

Back to the foot.

Constant pain despite PT, steroid injections, special shoes – didn't matter. I am introspective enough to know that beneath the surface, there was a lesson here. What I learned about myself is how incredibly shallow I really am. Take away my heels and my superpowers evaporate. In flats and ankle pants, I am so ordinary, I don't even see my reflection in a mirror. Can't wear ninety percent of what's in my closet. Everything involves at least a two-inch heel. Truly we are all only as strong as our weakest link. Didn't know that it was footwear for me.

It was time to "escalate" this issue. Joanna took me to the head ortho guy at the University Medical Center where she works. He examined my foot and asked me how much pain I was in prior to the implant.

Me: *None.*
Him: *You should never have joint surgery if you aren't in pain.*
Me: *Good to know. Can you fix it now?*
Him: *The time to have a second opinion is before surgery. But I will try.*

In the spirit of managing *expectations,* I reach into my purse and pull out a high heel.

THE SECRET TO HAPPINESS IS LOW EXPECTATIONS

Me: *I need you to get my foot back into this.*
Him: *No guarantee that your foot will look or work the same.*
Me: *I don't want any repercussions to being super active when I am old.*
Him: (looks right at me) *Isabel, you are sixty-one years old.*

In other words, that ship has sailed. I put the shoe and my ego back into the purse.

Two weeks later, Dr. Congeniality operated on my foot to fix the first operation I didn't need. Three days after that, Joanna and I moved into our new house downtown. Surgery and moving the same week. One star on Trip Advisor. I am on crutches for two weeks in a house full of boxes and I cannot do anything. I have to drink wine over the sink because I cannot carry the glass to the sofa.

The Grape Girls bought me a generous Uber Eats gift card mostly because they know Joanna's idea of cooking is four minutes on high in the microwave. Doesn't matter what it is.

Sidebar: Joanna had to make baked beans for a cookout once. It involved browning ground beef and an onion and opening four cans. The woman who routinely does ninety minutes on the Stairmaster with a band around her legs, burst into tears and collapsed five minutes in. I surely would have starved.
Then, Joanna and Scott are invited to a Superbowl party. Scott: *Sweetie Pie, the host wants us to bring our specialty dish to the party. Can you ask Isabel what that is? And can she make it for us?*

Turns out, immobility gives you lots of time to get restless. Once I could finally ditch the crutches and boot, I joined a gym. I'll stop here and admit to date, working out for me was two yoga classes a month. And not the hot yoga. My workout-with-a-buddy history went like this: When I quit The Corporation the second time, Dawn and I decided to be exercise buddies. She was the best partner ever. On Monday, Dawn would call and say, "*Let's go.*" On Tuesday, the carpet man might be coming so no dice. Wednesday, I have a writing deadline. Thursday, she's delivering something to the theater department at school. On Friday, I call to see when I can pick her up. "*Isabel, it's Friday… what's the point?*" We feel a little bit guilty, but we both agreed we had a long way to go before we looked as bad as Marie Osmond on *Dancing with the Stars*. Joanna says I need more cardio. If she means getting my heart rate up, I can do that at the Dillard's 75% off rack or Neiman's Last Call.

Back to the gym. Truth is, wandering into one for me feels a lot like visiting Home Depot, Starbucks, or the Texas State Fair. Puzzled at the crowds, not sure what the fuss is about, and anxious to leave.

Another pause to tell the little known story about wearing my pants backwards. I've always been thin. Shape is an entirely different matter. During a sales meeting, all dressed up, my coworker, Stephanie, points out that the slit at the hem of my slacks should be in front, not back. Hmmm. I went into the ladies' room and put my pants on the other way. Everyone thought it was a circus trick – to wear your pants both ways.

THE SECRET TO HAPPINESS IS LOW EXPECTATIONS

Seems a "perky bootie" is not in my genes. Or jeans for that matter.

Anyway…I had to do something. Every part of my body had kinks in it except my hair. So, yes, I not only joined a gym, but a fancy one. The kind made for princesses like me who don't sweat.

Once I did my mandatory orientation, they gave me the full court press on signing up for personal training. Met the boys for dinner. Told them I wasn't falling for that scam. They looked at each other and then at me.

Me: *Mommy joined a gym.*
David: *Well, that's great.*
Me: *They want me to buy all these personal training sessions but that's a scam. I'm just going to the complimentary one and then do stuff on my own.*
David: (long pause) *You. Loose in that gym? You don't know what the fuck you are doing…*

I didn't like his tone, but I had no rebuttal.

Enter thirty-something Jade. She is a Level 4 personal trainer, which means she is certified to train the injured, the old, and the ignorant. I checked every box. She is someone I love to hate. After never breaking a sweat all my life including during childbirth, Jade introduced me to my body, four Advil at a time. The initiation began with her asking me to do a squat and to her credit she kept a straight face. During our first formal session she asked me to sit on the floor and cross my legs. I bent my legs and put one knee over the other like they do in bathing suit ads. *"I mean Indian-style please,"* she said. The second session she told me I probably didn't need to wear perfume or do my hair and makeup.

I am mildly ill just before our workouts, anticipating the stop at Walgreens for more thermal patches. She's the only person who scares me more than my sister. Pushes me to the limit. Dead lifts, squats, lunges, bands, kettle bells, dumbbells, ropes, racks, machines.

Months later, Jade left my gym and began training sessions in her apartment. I followed her. Stockholm syndrome. She is quite a character – degrees in finance and kinesiology. A free spirit, tattoo sleeve, but remarkably deep. The antithesis of the personal trainer stereotype. At least the stereotype I always had. Bookshelves filled with actual literature in addition to psychology, anatomy, and homeopathy. She is starting a catering business because it came to her in a dream. Her paintings cover the wall. Her bike has a thousand miles on it. Jade's done some modeling. I saw a picture on *Instagram* where she is wearing an Indian headdress and nothing else. Feathers strategically placed. A pose in ripped tights and a midriff with chains. Sassy. Listens to podcasts on neuropsychology.

In between bottles of water and wiping myself down with towels, she counsels me on the folly of anxiety, the power of our minds, the discovery in every relationship, the presence of God. I think she's an angel.

I'm not so much of a stick figure anymore. Strong. Delighted. Turns out, it's fun to know *what the fuck you are doing*. With someone whose path you never would have crossed if it weren't for falling off a curb in high heels.

Starting over. Again.

*"When you're alone and life is making you lonely you can always go Downtown.
… don't wait a minute more
Downtown, everything's waiting for you."*
– Petula Clark/Tony Hatch

It started in January with having to put my beloved Labrador down. I don't think I cried as much for my mother and father at their funerals. This dog had been with me for fourteen years – and as I came to understand once he was gone – Champ was less a pet and more a service dog for me. It was like losing my shadow.

A few days after the dog event, I had foot surgery to put an implant in a hole in my toe joint. (See "Flats are for Quitters")

Upon returning to work a week later, dog-less and in a boot, I get called into the sales manager's office and told I am being given a new role. They want me to switch from wood and executive offices to healthcare furniture and what do I think about healthcare? *"I have absolutely no interest in it whatsoever,"* was my reply. It quickly became clear I wasn't really being asked. Like my mother used to say, *"If it was play, they wouldn't call it work."*

I did the best thing I could. I immediately asked for all the outlying territories. Austin, Memphis, Little Rock, Baton Rouge and New Orleans. Away from the drama of Houston and Dallas, with the added benefit of no one ever knowing exactly where I am. It was also a veritable point-making machine. I love points. I'm a Diamond and Platinum member. Greg says I'm a points-whore. I have enough Hilton points to probably get me at least two years of "assisted living" once that time comes. Just go from hotel to hotel on points.

But those points don't come cheap. The job is a lot of travel and there is so much to learn. Make no mistake – I love learning new things. Problem is, none of those interests include healthcare. It was more work than I ever imagined. Particularly since I had to act as if I give a damn about any of it. I always knew I could be a great actress but assumed a camera would be involved. To make matters worse, I was assured of a big bonus if I stayed in my former position. Not the case on the healthcare side. Slim bonus, if any. But on the plus side, more layoffs were looming, so maybe my corporate guardian angel was trying to protect me. God knows I need somebody doing that. And I can assure you, they're not on *Match.com*.

Trying to keep things chronological…springtime came, and I was seriously feeling the weight of my big house with a pool in the suburbs. David – my son the realtor – who fancies himself a life coach says to me, *"Mom, what are you doing surrounded by baby buggies and soccer matches? You need to move downtown. It's Disneyland and you can ride every ride…"* Never mind what that entails. He got top dollar for my house and found me a duplex in the "hood". Not in the heart of downtown, but a few exits up by the Katy Trail with all the cute shops and bars. My "realtor" left out the part about the crime and the traffic.

Moved end of July. Between June and July, downsizing was difficult. I had three attics in my suburban house. After the divorce, I moved everything to my new attic and for seven years, my history waited to be rediscovered. Time to sort through it. Found my elementary school report cards, first communion veil, programs from starring roles in high school plays, my graduation cap, diplomas, and the pregnancy test that turned out to be Gregory. Journals, yearbooks, mementos. Cried. Laughed. Drank wine.

Downsizing also meant getting rid of furniture. Worst moment was seeing my mother's dining room go out the door to charity. Decades of Thanksgivings were at that table.

> **Sidebar:** One year my mother declared during Thanksgiving dinner that she would not be serving mincemeat bars for dessert. The radio station she tuned into warned listeners that minces were an endangered species and begged

people not to contribute to their demise. It was a satire. But my mother didn't know it. She was convinced they were small furry animals — not chopped dried fruit and spices. All fourteen of us at the table put down our forks. *"Oh, they are making hats, shoes, and even purses out of them,"* she said. *"It's a terrible thing."* Dead serious. I don't remember who started it, but things got hysterical. People were laughing so hard they were sobbing. But the worst was my friend John who had his appendix out the previous Tuesday. I had to put him in the guest room to lie down because he thought his stitches were coming undone. We tried to carry on with normal conversations after that, but no one could keep a straight face.

Which is why I am so heartbroken that there seem to be no dining rooms anymore. Not in a duplex, or anywhere else I looked. So many memories at that table. It's an empty feeling starting over again. Again.

Joanna moved downtown with me. She was excited to be fifteen minutes from the hospital where she is a nurse (versus a one-hour commute) and I was ten minutes from our showroom. Everything is within walking distance or a short drive. Great, young energy and vibe. I can hardly get over myself for making this leap.

Once I was off crutches, it was time to get the house in order. Enter Patrick, the thirty-something handyman. Joanna thought he looked like a young Matthew McConaughey. Hiking boots, cargo shorts, and an Indiana Jones hat. If you remember *Murphy Brown*, he was my Eldon. He literally spent days and weeks with me. Moving furniture, touching up paint, fixing locks, switches, garage door openers, hanging pictures, etc. He was a godsend. Last time I ventured into Home Depot, I felt so lost; I cursed myself for ever getting divorced. No reason seemed big enough. With Patrick by my side, I can safely stay in the lightbulb aisle and leave the rest to him. But even Patrick has limits.

Our first week in the house, Joanna broke the French door hinge with her recycle bucket and she was afraid we would be raped since it was off the hinges and our back gate and fence are tipping over, so David had to come over with his gun that night and slept in the guest room. (*"What the hell is happening over there with you two?"*) I won't even tell you about the carbon monoxide alarms going off for no reason in August (later learning it was an electrical circuit thing that *"never happens"*) and I had the whole Dallas fire department here. I have a thing about firemen. These guys looked like the guys on the calendar. Glad I put lipstick and a small t-shirt on before they came. Then a giant wet spot appeared on the ceiling. I could go on, but you get the picture. Overall, love the house. Door hinge repaired. Roof leak and fireplace recently fixed. But now I think we have mice. Lots of tweaks but it's coming along. Looks very "downtown" or "uptown" depending. Big departure from the suburbs. Starting to feel at home.

Back at work, we have reached new lows in terms of our meetings. We've come a long way from black tie dinners at the Mansion on Turtle Creek and spas in Arizona. Our latest regional meeting was three interminable days in Houston.

We are asked to learn the new hundred-slide presentation on who we are, what we do, and why we do it. Every year a thinly veiled message with a slightly different angle. The corporate gods tell us we are transitioning and need to spread the newest gospel.

Me to Gabby: *I've transitioned with this company so many times, I don't know what bathroom to use.*
We both roar.

Then a manager got up to explain the newest format for account plans. He had an example. *"I will be passing out a dummy report from headquarters."*
Me: *Well, at least they are starting to admit it.*
Gabby and the peeps at our table got a snort out of that.

Meantime, eight hours of PowerPoint was mercifully interrupted by a team game with balls and baskets trying to prove something about agile behavior. We were put in teams of six. Gabby, me and four of the guys line up. We are asked to count the number of balls in our group. Gabby points to each man and counts 2-4-6-8. *"We have eight balls here,"* she says.
We cannot contain ourselves. Just shrieking. The game was over before it started.

THE SECRET TO HAPPINESS IS LOW EXPECTATIONS

Which is why they forbid us from sitting together at regional meetings.

For dinner, we arrived at a restaurant with picnic tables where we were told in advance to lock everything in our trunks. Our lunch was catered by one of the Millennial's friends. Looked like it came from Sam's Club. She didn't even bother to take the stuff out of the plastic containers. Second night was dedicated to one of the same Millennial's "causes" for literacy where we had to stuff bags with macaroni and laminate bookmarks while sitting on folding chairs.

Those of us who have been with The Corporation for twenty years or more (nine of us) just roll our eyes. They called us the "vintage people". I preferred "mid-century modern". I hoped I could hang on for four more years.

Back at the ranch, I decided I couldn't live with the busy granite counter tops, wine rack over the fridge and stone backsplash in the kitchen a minute longer. Hired a great contractor named David recommended by a friend. He arrived looking like he was someone you might try to help across the street. At least seventy-five years old. Brought all his sub-contractors – also in that age range. Fantastic workmanship. Didn't even need new cabinet facing because it all looked so good. Decided to have them do my shower upstairs too. Soon after they departed, I couldn't stop noticing the old carpet in the three bedrooms. Hired John, another diamond birthday guy who knew his way around every pad and pile. Perfect. They are a dying breed.

Note: In conversation, I learn that *all these men are younger than me*. Which is why I am now looking for someone in their forties.

And then the office needed painting. Jodi, (Greg's girlfriend at the time and now fiancée) who is a degreed interior designer, helped me pick out the right shade of green and insisted I use an ultra-high-end paint for $130 a gallon. Indeed, it looks like suede on the wall, but $130? Incidentally she has a pair of white booties with gold heels she wears quite often.
Greg: *You wear those cute boots all the time. Why don't you get them in other colors?*
Jodi: *Because they are Fendi and cost $2000.*

OH. I'm glad I stopped her at paint. In addition to being an interior designer, she is also a realtor. She "treats" herself when she sells a big property, so I say, "Well done." I'm trying to think if I even own anything that costs $2000. Like maybe my closet altogether.

And just when I paid off my Mastercard...the house again. If it were alive, I would say it was throwing a temper tantrum. Over the last four months I have replaced broken light fixtures, smoke alarm systems, locks, A/C parts, doors, attic stairs, and a blown down fence. I have so many repair vehicles parked in my driveway on a regular basis, all the neighbors are talking.

Truthfully, as unlucky as I am in love, the men in my life wearing tool belts and driving pickup trucks are the stuff a single girl's dreams are made of.

THE SECRET TO HAPPINESS IS LOW EXPECTATIONS

Julio – landscaping
David – renovations
Rick – paint
Matthew – plumbing
Gerardo – HVAC

Heath* – fence
*Heath is the exception to all the other 5 star guys. He does a great job on my roof but dragged his feet on my fence for so long I was getting furious. No trouble taking it down, just not enthusiastic about putting it back together. Julio was waiting to plant bushes but couldn't until the fence was finished. Our texts:

Me: *Julio, can you plant the rosemary bush from front porch to backyard sometime? Also, is that bush next to oak tree dead? Can you replace it? Why did it die? I am going to kill my fence man. Can you bury him in the backyard?*
Julio: *Sure. He's not done yet? Yes. Monday or Tuesday.*

That afternoon Julio *comes in person* to tell me he can't bury anyone in my backyard, but he will move the bushes Tuesday. People are funny.

Jason – electrical
Jason came to change a ballast in the laundry room. *While he was here*, my closet light fell out of the ceiling, the front door locked and would not reopen, locking us *inside* the house, and when I went to the pantry to get him a flashlight, that doorknob came off in my hand.

Jason: Let's just sit here a minute and let this settle down so I only have to go to Home Depot once.

I have spent more money this year than in the years when both boys needed college tuition. Which reminds me why I have to keep working.

That healthcare sales role…what more can they do to me? Demonstrating sleeper sofas, presenting recliners, learning CEUs on waiting room research. There was a day in March I distinctly remember. In a Memphis hospital transplant unit with actual patients all around me getting organs. I cannot get a blood test without asking for smelling salts. I left and waited in the lobby. My prayer went something like, *"Please wrap your arms around those people with no organs and please take me far, far away from tile floors and white coats."*

And the next day, the phone rang. It was Jim – the new wood category director saying there was a reorg going on and would I ever consider coming back to wood and my old territory? And my bonus was assured for March. And I could have Florida. And would I be a hostess at the wood incentive trip in Buenos Aires in February? I said I would consider it.
As if.

I was going down for the third time and a raft appeared. I would like to point out that this time God answered my prayer without sending me into surgery.

THE SECRET TO HAPPINESS IS LOW EXPECTATIONS

I was ecstatic. Regional management was not happy. My healthcare team wasn't happy either. After the "transition call" I felt a bit low.

Me to David: *I got that wood position. It was official yesterday.*

David: *That's great. Congratulations – it's what you need.*

Me: *It's just that I'm feeling guilty about leaving the team in a bad place. There's no one to take my job and I got some business started. It's going to be a burden on the team for a while.*

David: *Mom, there is no team in business. You want to know how to tell you're on a team? When everyone around you is either holding guns or wearing helmets.*

A fresh perspective.

Turns out I may need a helmet if I don't start paying more attention while I am driving. I was on my way to celebrate my new job with a Grape Girls lunch. I pulled out of the driveway, waved to my neighbors who were (oddly) standing in their driveway, and promptly backed into a police car. The driver's door. With the policeman inside. I swore he was not in my rear view mirror. I got out of my car.

Police: *Are you all right?*

Me: *No. I just hit a police car.*

Police: *I figured you didn't see me.*

Me: *What do we do? What do you need? My license? My insurance? (My phone number? Really not a bad looking officer…)*

Police: *Don't worry. The city will contact you.*

The neighbors stared at me.

Me: *"What a way to start the day."*

Them: *"He's here because our car got stolen out of the driveway last night."*
Me: *Oh.*
And off I go to my lunch. Damaged rear bumper. Cop car with his driver's door dented in.

I go around the block and park. I call Greg in a panic. He was more amazed that a policeman showed up for a stolen car. *"They don't even come if there's a murder. Unless it's a shooting spree. And no one from the city is coming, Mom. He just let you drive off. By the way what were you wearing?"* For the record it was my new mini halter dress. And no, the city never came. ⋀

Playing with Matches

"That's a lot of time spent looking fascinated."
– Jerry Seinfeld on online dating

*"I don't want no more of the cheese,
I just want out of the trap."*
– Glenn Barber, 1968 Country Music

After a final breakup from my long distance affair, I had no doubt my friends would come through with someone looking for someone just like me. I was dead wrong. Karen found me a prominent doctor and researcher – Derek – who took me to dinner in downtown Chicago, told me there was no God, that if there was one, he would be a reasonable facsimile; his ex-wife was a devil; and what did I feel about getting naked? Since I didn't show interest in being part of his "research" he left me on the street corner to find a cab as he walked away.

Lisa introduced me to Jonathon who ran a family business and was exceptionally handsome and charming. Problem was he had a medical checkup in between our second and third dates that showed a potential heart condition and I guess I made his heart beat too fast. He disappeared after making a third date.

One Saturday night, I was in my pajamas at 7:30 watching *Perry Mason* when the phone rang. It was Dr. Joyce, one of my closest friends, telling me to get dressed quickly and come to the bar where she and her husband were expecting Kelly to show up any minute. He is "in between" girlfriends, fifty-five years old, and owns all the real estate in an entire city in Texas. Been friends with Joyce's husband forever. I got dressed and arrived to find Kelly. A full-grown cowboy, with the boots, hat, belt buckle, and belly to go with it. He's showing Joyce a picture on his phone of an open wound on his mother's back, and what did she think that was? He wouldn't even acknowledge me. She had to physically turn him to look at me and remind him he knew my boys. There was a flicker of recognition.
Him: *Oh yeah. You got two good boys.*
Me: *Do you have any children?*
Him: *Yes. Three. All twenty-one years old now.*
Me: *Triplets?*
Him: *No.*
He showed me their pictures. One white, one Hispanic, one black.
He rescues me from having to comment.
Him: *Three different women. It was quite a year. I read the sex education manual back to front instead of front to back.*
He stops to howl and slaps me on the back. Then proceeds to follow some twenty-five-year-old girl around the bar.

THE SECRET TO HAPPINESS IS LOW EXPECTATIONS

I was glad I taped *Perry Mason*.

If this is what my "friends" thought of me, how bad could online dating be? After all, Karen found Mike and they are now living together and traveling the world. Jan met John; Kathy and Jim are still together. Although it started out a bit rocky, Joanna met Scott online.

Scott walked Joanna to her car after dinner. Joanna has a vanity license plate with her last name. JBolt.

Joanna: *Well now that you know my last name, you're going to find out I'm older than the age put on my profile.*

Scott: *You mean you are starting a relationship with a lie?*

Joanna: *Yes. And you are nowhere near six feet tall either.*

They just celebrated nine years.

Admittedly, Joanna did suffer through four or five bad "meetings." Like the one who spit when he talked. She claims she was soaked. I came home to find her clothes in a pile in the garage and her crying in the shower.

One night under the influence of Grey Goose, I put a few pictures together and wrote a profile. A missive to the online ocean of intimate strangers. As you read this, I'm an online dating survivor – offline for good but dealing with PTSD. What color ribbon should I wear? *Match, eHarmony, Elite Singles* – it didn't matter. My experiences were so noteworthy, I began to record these meetings in my scrapbook in case I was ever invited to open mic night at the Improv. Good thing I did. Here are the highlights of five years "playing with matches".

There was Jake, the international pilot who flew around the world eleven days a month, but when he heard I was moving twenty-five minutes away, said he was looking for someone within five miles of his house.

Then came Dr. Louis, a physician who talked for over an hour about his house renovation, infertility with first wife, his second wife's nerve disorder and death two months ago, his residency, diving accident, his practice and patients, his approach to diagnoses, dad's anaplastic cancer, his sister who worked at Lowes but is now an aesthetician and he will open med spa for her… I looked up his website afterward and the title was: "An active listener".

Shawn's wife left him five months ago. He was surprised. She wiped out his 401K and racked up $64K in credit card debt. Worked in his in-law's business in Baton Rouge but now getting his insurance license. He had a smoker's cough and whistled when he talked – I think dentures. From the time we sat down, he was rubbing his eye with a napkin. Said it was tearing up from cooking with jalapenos. No money, no job. The man's life is in shambles. He told me he's writing a book – *Reflections of a Life Well Lived*.

Jack was looking for life partner. We have a promising lunch, then he sends me pictures of a sleep clinic he is going to that night. Texted me, "I'm scared." Next day he hid his profile. Texts me, "Too much on my mind."

THE SECRET TO HAPPINESS IS LOW EXPECTATIONS

Mike sent me a "like" and wanted to get together. I sent one back. He was an executive and competitive tennis player. Looked good. We picked Saturday afternoon for coffee. He texted Saturday morning and wants me to meet him in a parking lot so he could see what I looked like first. Before he buys me coffee.
Me: *Mike it sounds like you have had some bad experiences. Me too. But I am NOT auditioning for you in a parking lot.*
Mike: *Okay. Bye.*

Jerry liked my pictures but messaged me for a full length photo to see if I had "cankles".

Rob wanted to meet me for lunch, but could I drive across town because he had a work appointment at 1:30 in the area. 11:30 sharp he says. Dress, makeup, hair…jump in the car and get there forty minutes later right at 11:30. 11:35 I get a text:
Rob: *Work crises…have to cancel.*
Me: *I drove from downtown Dallas. Would have appreciated more notice.*
Rob: *Oh. Sorry. Eat something and I will Venmo you the money.*
Me: *No thanks.*

(David: *Well, at least you are starting to make money on these clowns.*)

Grant is an architect. We immediately hit it off on texts. His sense of humor was fantastic. For the first time in a while, I was super interested. He had to cancel one date we planned to take a COVID test, but then he was cleared on Friday so we would meet Monday since I was in Austin for the weekend. Texted me

Saturday several times. Monday morning texts to cancel. *"Isabel, I met someone Saturday night and I think she is the one and I don't want to meet you knowing that."* Found the love of his life. One date.

Joe takes me out. Wants to see me again. Two days later texts me.
Joe: *Isabel, hope you had a good time last weekend with your friend and your daughter. Crossing my fingers for your dance competition next weekend.*
No daughter, no dance competition. He has mixed me up with another woman.

Brad. Seems nice. Talks through lunch about his kidneys and thirty-seven operations.
Me: *Are you okay now?*
Brad: *Kind of.*

Josh was a former Pittsburgh Steeler. He won't stop talking.
Him: *I guess I'm talking too much.*
Me: *Yes. Is there anything you want to know about me?*
Him: *I'd like to know everything about you.*
He keeps on talking.

One of my favorites was John, a professor in Waco. He called a couple times, but our schedules didn't agree. Always 10:15, 12, 1:45, 4:00, 6:30. Odd. Finally we settled on 4:00 one Saturday. I'm waiting at the restaurant. At 4:15, he calls and cancels. Explains since he lives ninety minutes away from Dallas, he is doing "stacked dating" and his 1:45 was pretty interesting – he was still with her, and the 6:30 woman was "hot" so could we do this next weekend?

Bob sold medical instruments for brain surgeons. He shows up to happy hour in scrubs and explains how he pretty much knows more about brain surgery than the surgeons since he shows them how to use his equipment. Asks me how online dating is going and I say not so good.
Bob: *Well, I had one woman at my house for a drink and when I turned around she was naked in my pool. Then another one took her pants off in my car while I went into the restaurant where I forgot my wallet.*
Me: *Why are you here with me instead of one of them?*
Bob: *I'm just saying you need to be much more aggressive if you want someone like me.*

Jerry was in Oil and Gas. Keeps making dates and cancelling and saying he is sorry. Then we make a new date. He forgets. Texts "Can't wait to see you on Saturday." Forgets.

Doug was a Canadian consultant. Liked him. Great first date. Then silence. After one week of silence, he texts. I answer the text thirty minutes later.
Him: *You took a while to reply, are you offended about something?*
Me: *Not at all. How are you?*
Him: (No reply for a week.) Then texts, he is going to Spain.
From Spain: *How is my pretty lady?*
Me: *Great. I'd love to see you again.*
Nothing for weeks.
Me: *Are you home from Spain?*

Him: *Yes*
Crickets.

Scott keeps me on the phone for forty-five minutes – wants to be sure we are compatible. Texts for a week. Asks me Monday for a date on Saturday – "Somewhere special at 6:00". Saturday arrives, no call. I texted at 5:15, all dressed and ready.
Scott: *I'm not going.*
Me: *You are kidding.*
Scott: *No. I had two horrible dates this week from that site, and I am finished.*

James is a lawyer. Was raising a kid from his first wife when he married his second wife who blatantly cheated on him. Wife #2 has two kids and $75k in credit cards. He buys her a house, pays off debt, puts both her kids through private high school $20k per year, gets them both a car, then college for one and two years for next one. He finally announces to his step kids that they need to start working. She says no, they don't have to… that is why she married him.
Me: *Why did you finally leave her?*
Him: *It was all good, but she started being mean to my daughter and that made me mad.*

Keith is an astronaut. He sent me five questions.
Question: *Where would you go if you had a week off?*
Isabel: *The moon.* (I get such a kick out of myself.)
No response for a couple days.
Me: *Do you laugh often?*

THE SECRET TO HAPPINESS IS LOW EXPECTATIONS

Keith: *NO. I have serious business.*

Craig is a neurosurgeon. Super cute. We text.
Craig: *Hello, Isabel, I'm a neurosurgeon. Would you be interested in meeting?*
Me: *I was really looking for a rocket scientist.* (couldn't help myself)
Craig: *Well, if we don't hit it off, I have a friend who is an astronaut.* (Hmmm – funny)
Me: *I like your sense of humor. Let's meet.*
Never calls or texts back.
Two months later…
Craig: *Hello, Isabel. I'm a neurosurgeon.*
He forgot we ever corresponded…

James, the SW Airlines pilot. We walked the Katy Trail. Twenty yards in, he says, "*Hold on a minute.*" Goes behind a tree to pee. Comes back zipping his pants. "*Ooh. That's better,*" he says.

Then there's the guy who texts me at eleven p.m. "*Wanna meet?*" I blocked him; the never-married attorney living with mom writing *James Bond*-type books; the man who went on for an hour about his washing machine and his mother's neuropathy; an anesthesiologist who sent me loving texts for two days after we had a drink then disappeared; and the poor guy who was a widower four months and talked about her all through breakfast including where he was throwing the ashes in June, but he wanted to be back on *Match* because that's where they met and it reminded him of her.

Eric gets first prize. Wanted to take me out. I said a drink would be fine. He calls and insists on dinner. Then adds a comedy club. Date was okay. I was charming. Knew he was not my type pretty early into the evening when I complimented his style, and he told me his coworkers think he is gay, but he is not. Of course he is. I stayed respectful and chatty. Wrote him a text the next morning and here is how that went:

Me: *Good morning, Eric. Thanks again for last night. I'm glad we got to know each other better. You have so many great qualities, but I don't think we are a match. You deserve someone who is crazy about you. I'm sure she'll find you soon. Take care. Isabel.*

Eric: *Isabel, I believe in a fair and balanced life. Your balance of the evening:*

Dinner: $50.40

Show and wine: $27.02

Total: $77.42

You can Zelle or use other means to send the payment to xxx

I do not think I should subsidize your journey

HE WANTED A DATE REFUND

I was going to send it, but Joanna said she would break all my fingers. Greg wanted his number so he could go beat him with a rubber hose.

It is my last date online. Mercifully, my subscription is lapsing. My Hail Mary pass is going to dinner with a (self-described) successful, reasonably good-looking man who I learn happened to have raised his two daughters in a certain suburb near Chicago. I mention I have a good friend, Andrea, who raised her sons in the same suburb.

THE SECRET TO HAPPINESS IS LOW EXPECTATIONS

His face freezes. You could see the puzzle pieces locking together. He puts down his fork.
Man: *Does Andrea have a son named Nick?*
Me: *Well, yes.*
Man: *That boy took my daughter's virginity after senior prom.*
Now, I fancy myself quite adept in every social situation. No longer.

At this point I am grasping the essence of an old Texas saying: *There's only so much time you can spend fishing before you throw a stick of dynamite in the water.*

I'm done.

To be fair, some of the guys were good men. Responsible, successful, smart. I wish I could have fallen in love with even one of them, but I didn't feel anything – or rather I did. Joanna said if I grit my teeth when they held my hand, it probably was a bad sign. The other characters deserved an invoice from me for the mock therapy sessions. So few ever asked me a single question. I could have been in the witness protection program. For the most part, I felt like the little girl who walks through the farm and says, *"There must be a pony somewhere."*

And then there was this…you remember Karen – my mentor and self-proclaimed "fun fairy" from Chicago. She calls. There is a special Mediterranean cruise happening next summer. It is for the American Society of Aesthetic Plastic Surgeons, and she is a featured speaker. I have written for some of the surgeons attending. Tells me the cruise will be spectacular. I have to go. I see the itinerary. Yes, I have to go. And *I have a year to find someone to go with me*. How difficult can that be? Answer: Very. All that online dating yielded exactly *no one*. My love life was in free fall. I took Greg with me.

We started in Rome for four days. Then boarded the ship bound for Capri, Sicily, Malta, Greece, Croatia, Montenegro, Slovenia, and finally Venice. It was going to be epic. Except *everyone* was there with their wife, husband, boyfriend, or girlfriend. As we set sail, I started feeling like a sad country song and looked for a big glass of whiskey. That quickly changed. Not once or twice, but about a *dozen times* during the cruise people assumed Greg and I were a *couple*. He of course, was mortified. We would pass by, and people would whisper. He had his eye on one of the Asian girls in the string quartet. Made me follow behind him by twenty feet.

My favorite line of the whole cruise:
We are at dinner. A doctor's wife is sitting next to me and across from Greg. She leans over to me and whispers, *"How long have you and Greg known each other?"* I leaned in. *"Twenty-six years."*

All I can say is if he is twenty-six and I am sixty-two and people think he is my boyfriend…there's a lot of living yet to do, my friends.

All aboard. ⋀

The Corporate Package

"Well, I've been livin' in fast forward...
now I got to rewind real slow."
– Kenny Chesney

My favorite pandemic *Instagram* post:
Article: *Scientists find 33 creatures living in a cave that was sealed off for five million years.*
Random comment: Seal that cave back up and WALK AWAY. This is NOT the year, man.

It was 2018, and I needed something to read on the flight home from visiting my distributor in San Antonio. They had a library in the breakroom, so I picked out a self-help book. The book talked about committing to a "word of the year." My first one in 2018 was "trust". Followed in 2019 by "acceptance". Both total failures. At the end of 2019, I declared "anxiety" would be my word for the yet-to-be-experienced 2020, since that happens to come quite naturally to me. Given the high stakes that would befall us in 2020, makes one wonder if I was clairvoyant.

In any case, I am happy to report I nailed that one. Living up to "anxiety" all year was such a complete success, I am declaring that game over and starting a new one. Hereafter, I propose giving the year a name in *retrospect*. 2020 was a whopper, but I haven't figured out a tagline big enough. I don't think anyone ever will.

It began in January with me on a mission to find a rescue dog. Turned out finding my match was eerily similar to online dating. Joanna, David, and Greg all took turns going with me to shelters. None of the dogs were quite "right," and the ones I thought I liked…I went back, and they were gone. At one point so many dogs I liked disappeared, Joanna said I should volunteer to simply walk through overcrowded shelters to accelerate adoptions. Mid-January I found Tank – who was not the breed, color, or age I wanted. But exactly what I needed. Joanna talked me into him. I probably should take her on dates with me.

I call Tank a *Lambador*. He is black and part pit bull, part lab, and part lamb. No jumping, chewing, barking, accidents…just perfect. Sits at my feet at the computer. I swear he has a human face. Never thought I would recover from losing Champ, and while he will never be replaced, I could eat this "Pittie" with a spoon.

In February, I went on that Argentina corporate award trip. Now, this harkened back to the good old days when The Corporation was my sugar daddy. What a once-in-a-lifetime experience. Beef for breakfast, lunch, and dinner. Tango lessons, bike rides, polo matches, architectural walking tours, the

THE SECRET TO HAPPINESS IS LOW EXPECTATIONS

Four Seasons Hotel...perhaps The Corporation was turning a corner, and I could last a couple more years. But wait. There was a brick wall around that corner. We returned February 28. On March 13, the world shut down.

The Dallas showroom where I officed (and one of the reasons I moved downtown) eventually closed down. Management instituted zoom calls for our region to inspire some synthetic form of connection. Cannot really blame them. Separated us into groups of twelve. Every Monday, we had a Zoom call to meet virtually and say what we did on the weekend and what business activities we thought were pertinent for that week. We were asked to vote on what to call that. I kept my mouth shut. The vote was in. Mindshare Mondays.

I remember feeling a pit in my stomach. All the comradery we shared at the regional office evaporated. No one's fault, really, but the calls were beyond meaningless. Comic Brian Regan once described someone going on and on with no substantive point: *"You've managed to follow nothing...with less..."* And that is how it went.

Meanwhile, one weekend BLM decided to riot near where I live and were literally a couple miles away marching up the expressway burning things. On the call that following Monday, our sales manager began with an I-hope-all-of-you-are-okay kind of speech. When it came to my turn to share, I simply said the social climate was making me think of getting a gun for protection. Two hours later, I get a call from my EVP (whom I love).

Me: *I'm so happy to hear your voice. To what do I owe this honor?*
EVP: *First, you are not in trouble.*
Me: *Of course I'm not. I haven't left the house in a week.*
EVP: *I have to call because a formal complaint has been made to HR about you. It seems one of your teammates feels threatened by you and your interest in guns.*
Me: *WHAT? (I paused just long enough to stop myself from saying I would like to strangle this person, hence giving HR ammunition – no pun intended) Does this person know about the second amendment? And that they are living in Texas? Move them to California. And another thing, after twenty-eight years with this company, if I darkened HR's door with some of the REAL issues** I experienced – I promise you I would OWN the enterprise by now. That complaint better be off my record by tomorrow.*

He never posted it; he agreed it was bogus. Never told me who it was but said that the person needed to "grow up." I chalked it up to one of the pussy millennials on my Zoom team and never shared another story.

**In the late 1980s, my boss at The Corporation told me despite the fact that I contributed the largest dollar volume to the region, he would be splitting up the bonus I earned with the men who had wives they were supporting at home. The reason? Jeff and I were "DINKs" – double income, no kids. True story.

Meantime, I did get a gun. David took me to the Fort Worth gun show.
David: *Mom, we are about to land in the people zoo. Except you get to walk inside the exhibits.*

THE SECRET TO HAPPINESS IS LOW EXPECTATIONS

It was quite a scene.

The fear and hysteria that accompanied COVID-19 was felt far and wide. So many were adversely affected physically, economically, emotionally, mentally. Which is why I am reluctant to admit that our family basically thrived. The worst part about it was the continued frustration with the government's poor communication, contradictions, and mandates. Thankfully, we live in Texas where the lockdowns were relatively short-lived.

Joanna, at the hospital treating folks with head and neck cancer was relieved to temporarily be home for a month and when she returned, patients were too scared to come in, so her days were less hectic. Rather let their cancer grow than possibly get COVID. So sad. Reasonable people turning irrational.

David had his best year in real estate and Greg was so euphoric not to be on a plane four days a week, consulting all over the planet, that he could barely contain his joy. I went to the gym, to massages, to restaurants, flew to New York and Minnesota and Little Rock. Even attended a fancy wedding with 150 people at a landmark hotel, no masks. We were traced. No one got COVID.

Greg was exposed at poker parties, bachelor parties, and pool parties. Everyone caught it but him. He even dated who he referred to as his "COVID buddies." One called after a long weekend and told him she was positive.
Greg: *Mom, there is no way I don't have it. She and I...*

Me: *TMI.*
Yet, negative.

David and Kristen moved in together a mile from me and stayed healthy despite her being at the hospital in her last year of medical school. This was all prior to the vaccine, so all I can say we were in an invisible bubble of protection and grateful for that. And all that time, I cannot explain it, but I was calm and not worried about getting it. My anxiety was more about the uncertainty of when would be getting back to normal.

My brother on the other hand rode around in his car in an N95 double mask. Alone.

Common sense did not always prevail even in Texas. David went to get his driver's license renewed at the DMV that summer and came home in a white-hot rage when he waited three hours only to be told they couldn't take a copy of his birth certificate – needed the original.

David: *I'm sitting here watching people who all look like characters out of a Tim Burton movie. The building is 100K square feet – way too big for the work they do. Something doesn't add up. Mom, it's a human portal. They're housing people that just crashed into this planet an hour ago from outer space and are pushing them out the back door. None of them are from here. And they are asking for MY original birth certificate?*

Meanwhile there is a lady in a Ford Fiesta with a whistle holding a clipboard out her window with times on it going up and down the parking lot telling people when they are allowed to get in line. Thirty minutes before your time, you can stand in line in 105 degrees and then they take your TEMPERATURE, which is also going to be 105 degrees, at the door to see if you have COVID. Fuck this.

And he left. But not before the man parked next to David backed his trailer hitch into the car behind him and another driver sideswiped the same car. At the DMV.

And then it happened. The Corporation offered a generous early retirement package. I had to think about it over the weekend. Why did I hesitate? Because I have a strong aversion to walking through doors labeled "unknown." Also, despite all the jokes and complaints about corporate life, this was my tribe. Corporate headquarters, the regional office, my distributors—I felt "known." It was always a safe place to land. Not to mention all the intermittent fun together.

Came to my senses and accepted the package along with eight of my fellow "VINTAGE" colleagues. The mass exodus shocked the region.

My last day at The Corporation was September 8th. Twenty-nine years. Although not difficult to believe, the last call of my career was to the I.T. help desk with whom I was always on a first name basis. I couldn't set my permanent out of office. *("This never happens.")* Computer would not shut down. Almost poignant. Was on the phone with Raj for one hour trying to detach from my computer. Fitting closure.

But…

A strange thing occurred after I officially left The Corporation. It had been my home for three decades. The euphoria lasted about two days. They called it a "retirement package" and that bothered me because I am in no mindset to be ready to retire.

I felt like I was drifting…

I don't eat fast food. But when I'm feeling a little depressed or overwhelmed, I go to KFC. I get the original recipe breast, green beans, mashed potatoes, gravy, and a roll. Then I sit in the parking lot and eat all of it. Thirty-two napkins are involved, but I still have grease in between every finger. Joanna says to kick off my flip flops and rub that into my heels. Elbows too. I found myself there four weeks in a row. Red flag.

My close "vintage" friends who really did retire were fussing over grandchildren, looking for senior discounts, gardening, trading in high heels for "sensible" shoes, taking naps. I didn't identify with any of it. Naps maybe. But still.

My friend, Megan recommended I order a book entitled *Expectation Hangover* by Christine Hassler. It was a great book for me since I have a chronic case of it. This led to some podcasts, books, and fleeting moments of self-discovery. Because of my browsing, I began getting all kinds of "life coaching" feeds on my phone. Apparently it was quite simple. If I… "Tended to my own vibration," "Soothed my inner child," "Healed my

THE SECRET TO HAPPINESS IS LOW EXPECTATIONS

stacked wounding," and "Realized how 'me being me' would lead to a bad ass breakthrough," I would arrive at self-actualization. I could go on. But it gives me muscle spasms. Evidently, neither self-absorbed nor self-aware, I had a lot of work to do.

Another friend bought me a "reading" so I could gain some clarity. It involved a questionnaire, an astrological chart, crystals, some burnt sage – I made an appointment.

Me to Joanna: *I had my reading today with Nicki.*
Joanna: *How did it go?*
Me: *It was really interesting.*
Joanna: *What did she say?*
Me: *Well, lots of good stuff. I have a strong feminine aura and nurturing heart. And my chart said I was born under a lucky star.*
Joanna: *When is that supposed to start?*
My sister is sensitive that way…

While I went searching for answers in my quest for self-discovery, I did find out there IS a certain dollar amount that can buy happiness. Which is always good to know. Turns out, for me, it is $609. At Lowes. I bought myself a garage refrigerator and I still get a rush every time I open the door. Never had enough space, but now I could fill a brand new fridge with all my cooking. It's "my jam" as the kids say.

The other purpose for bringing that up is to share a story demonstrating the interesting and comical people that surround us.

I bought the fridge on Halloween. The appliance sales lady waiting on me was dressed in costume. Horns, pitchfork, red pants, but with giant white foam ball around her torso.
Man waiting behind me: *What are you supposed to be?*
Lady: *Well, I am a snowball's chance in hell.*
Man: *You forgot the Dallas Cowboys hat.*
Hilarious.

I was "retired" for exactly eight weeks.

The CEO of one of our distributors called me. Brenda and I have been close friends/business associates for twenty years. Regardless of my role, my territory always included her firm. Over the years, she launched herself from a sales rep to VP to President and eventually CEO of four dealerships. I love her. She is a force of nature. Next thing I knew I was in her butterfly net.

The dirty little secret of my career is I never felt any particular affection for the industry in which I spent almost thirty years—the people, yes, not the job. I had left and come back three times. Reminded me of "Hotel California"… *"You can check out anytime you like, but you can never leave."* I really preferred to leave it for good, but on the other hand, I had no idea where I was going. Brenda played the role of *The Godfather* and made me an offer I couldn't refuse.
Three days a week, VP of Marketing Communications, generous salary, visit her locations when it's convenient, do only the things I like, have an assistant – well, Hollywood wasn't

THE SECRET TO HAPPINESS IS LOW EXPECTATIONS

exactly knocking on the door. Nor was Mr. Right anywhere to be found to whisk me away...so, I said "yes" to the mess. It was a perfect bridge to keep me feeling sharp, vital, and somewhat connected. And psychologically safe.

If you are following, *I took a test drive divorce, and now a test drive retirement.*

My part time job was not without drama.
Barely recovered from Joanna's birthday and David's wedding and here comes NeoCon – the annual convention for our industry in Chicago at the Merchandise Mart. Thousands of folks in the industry attend. Part of my marketing job included arranging a rooftop celebration for our clients and partners attending the show. I chose a fancy hotel on Michigan Avenue overlooking the river. Signed the contract a year in advance to save our special spot.

Brenda and I arrived the evening of the reception at 5:00 p.m. *No, no, NO.* It is nothing like the pictures. We had fifty people coming at 5:30 and the part of the rooftop that was "ours" was the size of a one-car garage. I assumed we had the whole rooftop. Panic. Great view, but if more than four people came we were in trouble. Oh, and the open bar was missing. We were to flag down waitresses doing the other three parties on the roof that evening.

You should know, Brenda has an established a reputation as leading a faith-based organization. I was counting on her mercy as people started coming in dozens. It was becoming increasingly impossible to greet people and smile through my nervous breakdown. Lo and behold at 5:45 the city got pitch black. All our phones went off. Tornado in downtown Chicago – which incidentally, *"never happens."* An answered prayer. God's timing was definitely improving. We had to evacuate. What luck. The manager is screaming for us to go to the "Fire Room." It was a room below, off the main bar with a fireplace, but Brenda heard "fire escape" and started yelling back at him that her guests were not going from a roof to a ladder. The whole situation was out of control. Once the tornado passed over us, and we were settled in this lovely room with drinks in hand, she pulled me aside.

Brenda: *Isabel, you know, these types of scenarios that happen quite regularly to you are a lot funnier when they don't involve me.*

I promised to keep a low profile, but I couldn't help myself the next day. We were standing in a group of designers and the manufacturer was presenting a new chair. It was their hallmark piece for the show, featured in the front window of the showroom. The fabric was an embroidered montage of all the endangered species. The designers were enchanted. I studied it, then whispered to Brenda…

I don't see any straight white men represented.
Brenda under her breath: *I am going to throw you through this window.*
It was worth it.

THE SECRET TO HAPPINESS IS LOW EXPECTATIONS

I wanted to do an excellent job for Brenda but by the end of 2023, it was harder and harder to go through the motions. It was evident to me that I was stalling.

Looking back, it is crystal clear how desperate I was to hang onto the familiar even if it was no longer serving me. Maybe it never did. Wrong movie, wrong script? Throughout my thirty-plus-year career, I often felt my piece didn't fit the puzzle. But it doesn't matter now. The time for pondering that question has long since passed. Don't get me wrong. There were great people, lifelong friendships, fun times, even some success. Meaning and purpose? Not really. But was there supposed to be? No one else seemed overly concerned about that.

In high school I performed lead roles in the drama club's productions. I loved theater. Fancied myself quite an actress. However, as part of the curriculum there were "improv days" where you act out scenes without a script. Beyond terrifying for me. I always called in sick those days. And now the improv was happening in real life. Retirement was inevitable.

No calling in sick for that. ⋏

I'm Suing Gabby for Secondhand Stress

"No good deed goes unpunished."
– Clare Boothe Luce

"There cannot be a stressful crisis next week. My schedule is already full."
– Henry Kissinger

You can safely assume that when you have a best friend for close to forty years, there will be quite a history. Gabby and I shared our professional and personal lives simultaneously creating a steady stream of episodes. Some hilarious, others heart-rending. I am the Lucy to her Ethel. You have already heard our battle cry:

"If I can just make it through this week..."

Call it a mantra. Call it a motto. Other times, a prayer. One of us will say it to the other roughly fifty-two weeks a year. I am the 911 operator when...

She thinks she's pregnant (again)
Custody battles start with husband #1
Infidelity happens with husband #2
I have to put her pantyhose on her after an all-nighter at a sales meeting
Her daughter had a brain tumor (she is A-okay now)
An IRS letter comes
The dining room ceiling collapses from a plumbing leak
She falls off her roof cleaning gutters
She goes in for gallbladder removal and winds up in ICU with hours to live…

This list is just a representative sample. But you get the picture. Despite her predicaments, Gabby is resilience personified. The problem is, she always calls me first. Then hangs up, finishes work or goes home… relieved and on her way. I hang up, have a panic attack, and cannot sleep for a week. She bounces into action. I splat and reverberate. Secondhand stress. It's a killer.

So, it's the end of October 2021. I am balls-to-the-wall that week getting ready to fly to Little Rock for a speaking engagement and gala and all the activities that go along with my post-retirement, "part time" job.

It's nine a.m. Gabby calls. Tells me she thinks she is having a stroke.

Let me preface this by saying although we talk daily, I did not speak to her for three days prior because she made me mad. She had been sick a couple times recently from overdoing things and then she starts to dig a stump out of the yard in eighty-five-degree weather, finally giving up. She is sixty-eight, but won't stop mowing lawns, climbing through her attic hunting vermin, planting 600 begonias, pulling 200-pound oriental rugs through the house...you get the picture. And now stumps.

Selfishly, I am her best friend and medical power of attorney and emergency room Uber driver, so I am involved. Not yet over her almost dying in 2015 from the malpractice gallbladder removal where the surgeon cut her common bile duct, remember that? (See *"What's love got to do with it?"*)

Back to the call:
She repeats she thinks she is having a stroke. Last thing she remembers is cutting down tree branches (see what I mean?). I do the drill...*Can you raise your arms? Stand on one leg? Are you numb? Dizzy? Look in the mirror – is your smile crooked? What are your kids' names?* She seems lucid. She is not slurring her words. I tell her to go to the doc-in-the-box at the corner and call me from there. With no other symptoms, I presume she might be having a panic attack. Probably because at this point I am projecting.
I wait. And wait. She's not calling. I call her. She picks up. I can tell she is in the car. She cannot find the doc-in-the-box by Kroger – the Kroger she goes to twice a day. The Kroger that puts out a silver alert if they don't see her by noon.
Gabby: *I think I had a stroke.*
Me: *I know but go inside the doc-in-the-box and I'll meet you.*

Gabby: *It is not here. I think I had a stroke.*

Now I am scared. And mad I told her to drive. I tell her to turn around, go three blocks back home. I will be there right away. Made the thirty-minute drive in ten minutes. She opens the door.

Gabby: *You got here so fast.*

Me: *There was no traffic.*

Gabby: *You got here so fast.*

Me: *I got worried when you were driving to doc-in-the-box.*

Gabby: *I never drove anywhere this morning.*

Me: *Let's sit down.*

She looks good but a little dazed. I call 911. They ask me the same questions I asked her earlier. They send the fire department and paramedics who arrive in five minutes.

I have to stop here to say I have NEVER seen men in real life that looked like these five. Something out of Chippendales. Tall, strong, little stubble, big chests, flat tummies, nice butts. I almost forgot why they were there. They put Gabby in a dining room chair and ask questions while they are doing vitals.

Fireman: *What is your birthday?* She gets it.

Fireman: *Address?* Not sure.

Fireman: *What day is it?* Thursday. (It's Tuesday.)

Gabby: *Isabel, take our picture with these men.*

Fireman: *What year is it?* 2020 (No.)

Gabby: *Let's get a picture with these men.*

Fireman: *Are you on medication?*

Gabby: *Just vitamins.* (Wrong.)

Gabby: *Isabel, you should take our picture with these men.*

Fireman: *You can come to the station when you feel better, and we'll take a picture then.*

THE SECRET TO HAPPINESS IS LOW EXPECTATIONS

Me: (Mind bubble) *Oh, someone's coming to the station, but I am going alone.*
Fireman: *Do you know who the President of the United States is?*
She pauses. *Obama?*
Fireman: *No, it's Biden.*
Me: *Wish we all could forget.* (Men got a real kick out of that.)
Fireman: *Let's take a ride to the hospital.*

Outside, several neighbors who all know Gabby are waiting by the ambulance, worried. I asked Dorothy, her next door neighbor and good friend for her cell number so we can communicate. She is so frantic; she tries but cannot remember it. Her husband can only remember the first three numbers. I give them mine. They can call me later. I can only deal with one compromised person at a time and there's only one ambulance. And off to the hospital in the ambulance Gabby went with me following behind.

In the ER, they get to work and within fifteen minutes she has a CT scan, X-ray, urine, bloodwork, and an ER doc and a Neuro doc visit. Impressive. She looks at me after they leave and asks why she isn't undergoing any tests and where are the doctors? Literally cannot remember anything that happens or any answers I give for more than five seconds. She asks the same questions over and over like a sick parrot. Every twenty seconds, it starts all over with… "*Isabel, walk me through this morning to connect the dots.*" No matter what I say, she says, "*I think I had a stroke,*" then, "*Should we call the kids?*" "*How did I get here?*" "*Where are the doctors?*" "*When will they test me for a stroke?*" "*Did the* neighbors come out?" "Do I have makeup on?" Then back to *"Connect the dots."* Same eight sentences for six hours. I am going out of my mind with fear and frustration. At Hour 3, a second Neuro doc comes in and asks to see me in the hall.

Me: *What is wrong with her?*
Doc: *We do not think it is a stroke. We think it is TGA. Transient Global Amnesia. It is quite uncommon. Usually lasts less than twenty-four hours and they have no recall of the time. But also, no side effects. And it rarely recurs.*
Me: *What causes it?*
Doc: *Physical over exertion, head trauma, violent sex…*
Me: *Well, I don't see any head trauma.*
Doc: *Probably something physical.*
Me: *Okay, I am stuck on the "usually" twenty-four hours. She is driving me crazy with the same questions. Can't you give her a sedative?*
Doc: *No, because we cannot have her sedated for the EEG we're going to do. You will just have to be patient; I know it's difficult.*
Me: *In that case, it will be less difficult if you sedate me, and I know exactly how much Xanax I need.*
Doc: Smiles but ignores me. *What is your relationship to the patient?*
Me: *I am her best friend and also medical power of attorney.*
Doc: *Does she have a DNR?*
Me: Smile but ignore him. *Not sure, but I would like to request a pillow.*

After the EEG, it is 4:30 and I am whipped. She has not stopped talking since nine a.m. This is not unusual, but in general, she repeats herself less. I tell Gabby I'll be back soon and I go home to feed the dogs. Joanna comes home and I am crying. I

THE SECRET TO HAPPINESS IS LOW EXPECTATIONS

had called her earlier about Gabby. Now I have to go back to the hospital. Joanna goes into her no-nonsense-nurse-mode.
Joanna: *Sit down here and start writing every question she keeps asking along with the answer. Hand her the notebook when you get there and stop talking to her. Tell her to read her own FAQs.*
Brilliant.

When I arrive at the hospital at 6:30, Gabby tells me she is glad I found her. She doesn't know how she got to the hospital. *Asks me where I have been all day.* I want to kill myself.
Gabby: *Isabel, I think I had a stroke.*
Me: I hand her the book. *Page one.* It worked.

Bottom line: She stays overnight for observation. I call her the next morning at seven a.m. with the fear of God in me that she will ask me about connecting dots. But all she says is… *"Who can get any rest around here when they're in my room every fifteen minutes?"*
She was back.
I, on the other hand, was out of Xanax.

One week later: Gabby gets on Facebook and joins a support group for TGA people.
Me: *So, you are engaging with people who don't remember their experience to share it?*
(She is so excited about everything she is learning. Has read thirty pages of people's stories.)
Two weeks later: Gabby tells me she wants a second opinion.
Me: *You don't remember the first opinion.*

She calls the University Medical Center. Gets an appointment with the neuro doc.

The appointment is in the Neuro clinic. Doc is a specialist in Alzheimer's but also treats Parkinson's, MS, Dementia, and TGA. Nurse escorts Gabby back to room and introduces herself.
Nurse: *My name is Memory.*
Gabby: *You are kidding.*

Doctor does cognitive exam first, naming months backwards, deducting seven from one hundred consecutively, then asks Gabby to remember four words and he will test her at the end of the exam for recall. The words are house-dog-yellow-27. Does physical exam…walking forward, backward, joint response, skin pricks. Says all looks good.
During meeting with neuro doctor Gabby comments on how much more prevalent TGA is than reported.
Doc: *It actually is very uncommon.*
Gabby: *That's not what my Facebook support group says.*
Doc: *Oh.*
Gabby: *I'm a little worried about getting it again.*
Doc: *No, it rarely recurs.*
Gabby: *There's lots of stories in my Facebook group that said it does.*
Having lost the argument to his opponents on Facebook, the doctor goes to the door.
Doc: *Take care. Memory will be in with your paperwork. Goodbye.*
Gabby stays on the exam table.
Doc: *Anything wrong?*

THE SECRET TO HAPPINESS IS LOW EXPECTATIONS

Gabby: *Doctor? YOU FORGOT the recall test. House-dog-yellow-27.*

I was not there, but fairly sure it took everything he had to not let his own brain explode.
I assume a special warning label is in her chart.

Six Saturdays and a Sunday

> *"Life is your artwork. Create it.
> No one else can do it for you."*
> — Max Ehrmann

> *"You know you are retired when you
> resent getting dressed for a nail appointment."*
> — Gabby

It is February of 2024, and I am retiring for real this time. Sort of. I am suffering from an extreme case of cognitive dissonance. Which means I am well aware of reality but desperately seeking an alternative. I don't want to be sixty-six. It's weird being the same age as old people. I got a birthday card that said, *"How old would you be if you didn't know how old you were?"* My answer: Thirty-four. So, I don't tell anyone my age. But now I have to start lying about my children's ages and it's hard to do all that math in my head.

Years ago, Oprah had Tina Turner and Cher on her show. At the time they were sixty-eight and sixty-one, respectively.
Oprah: *How do you feel about aging gracefully?*
Cher: *It sucks.*
Oprah: *But what about all the wisdom?*
Cher: *Fuck wisdom.*
I like Cher.

The problem is I am having my adolescence fifty years late. I mentioned earlier that I am one of those late bloomers. Really, really late. Like I am in my sixties, and I haven't done my thirties yet. I am Benjamin looking-for-the-pause Button. Preferably before the fourth quarter arrives. Gabby tells people that when she met me in my twenties, every time I bent over, a rosary fell out of my ass. She was the wild child. Now I want my turn. On the other hand, there is a reason you do your thirties in your thirties. Like staying up past the *Ten O'clock News*.

I told a friend I was feeling so off balance – no husband, no replacement, no job, boys on their own… "*Everything that defined me is gone,*" I said. He listened. *"Why are you letting 'things' and circumstances define you?"* he asked. Now there's something worth pondering. Without a doubt.
I never *expected* retirement would be like this. I pictured something completely different. After a lifetime of making sure everyone was taken care of, they are all doing fine. I'm just not sure how to take care of myself. No one to pour myself into except me. Being in charge of yourself with no one depend-

THE SECRET TO HAPPINESS IS LOW EXPECTATIONS

ing on you that you can blame – that's a lot of responsibility. I thought I would have figured things out by now.

Suzanne says that if I was cut open someone would find a very big, very tight spring. I can't help it. I start every morning reading my *Jesus Calling* prayer book. I end every day with *Dateline*. Scriptures in the morning, murder at night. So, I've got that covered. What about in between?

Since I am running out of runway, I spend more time at the gym. If I stay strong, I might postpone the walk-in tubs, scooters, Depends, and wearing a life alert. Speaking of runways – David calls.

David: *What are you doing?*
Me: *I am on the Stairmaster listening to a podcast.*
David: *About what?*
Me: *An interview on "How to participate in your own unfolding."*
David: *Oh. So, you are learning how to deconstruct the plane on the way down?*
Children are such a comfort.

I got my first Social Security check. By the time I ran the numbers for skin care, Botox, hair color, waxing, manicures, collagen and wine – there was $250 left. Which is why I am looking for a part-time job in either an upscale salon or a plastic surgery office.

Despite the gym membership and the lotions and potions and enhancements from the neck up, I look down and see my mother's hands. Everything is a little looser and a little lower. I prefer not to wear glasses at all when I look in the mirror. Slowly going blind is a great filter. But sight sure comes in handy for everything else.

Case in point: On my last business trip I grabbed one of those individually wrapped makeup remover towelettes out of my suitcase and wiped my face. It smelled different, so I dug it out of the wastebasket, put on my glasses and discovered I just used *Summer's Eve* on my face. By the way, it did a pretty good job removing makeup.

Back to my retirement. In the late 1990's, early 2000's, I went to a therapist. Her name was Judy and I loved her. She had a way of removing layer upon layer of the proverbial onion until I could clearly see the root. Of course this had to be stopped. Plus I didn't need a therapist. So, I only went once a year, mainly to see if her questions changed so I could justify my clinging to what wasn't working. One of her proclamations resonated deeply. Probably because it is true. *"You are a production junkie… addicted to doing versus being."*

Now I am looking for my next "hit."

After living so many years ahead of each day, suddenly I'm as fragile as a Fabergé Egg. I've been removed from the assembly line. So I call my life coach, who, you will remember, also happens to be my son.

David: *You are here. You've arrived. You worked your whole life and now you've made it.*

THE SECRET TO HAPPINESS IS LOW EXPECTATIONS

Me: *I'm not sure how to do that.*

David: *Just put your ass in an innertube and float down the Lazy River. You are IN the river. YOU are NOT the river. Not the current. Not the course.*

Judy would be proud of him.

My real therapist is Travis who masquerades as a hairdresser. I've known him for twenty years. He is a work of contemporary art: curly blond hair tucked under an Irish cap, barrel-chested, wrapped in a vinyl apron with skulls on it and black high top sneakers. Carries an MCM bag covered in spikes. Has one in every color. These days, I have to see him every three weeks or I look like Cruella Deville. Travis is also my stylist for Karen's socialite parties and family weddings,* my anchorman for politics (he actually reads Supreme Court opinions) and all things entertainment (he knew the verdict before Johnny Depp.)

> ***Sidebar:** David's wedding day. Travis arrives at my home early to do my hair, makeup and zip up the dress he chose for me to wear. We are upstairs. Downstairs the eight groomsmen arrive, tuxedos in hand along with the photographer. It seems to be getting loud down there. I summon Best Man, Greg, to remind him of the Catholic altar they will all be standing on in less than two hours. He assures me there is one bottle and one toast going on. I see Travis and Greg's eyes meet and look away. I assume since I helped raise most of the boys "toasting" downstairs, they are still afraid of me. I was wrong.

We are ready. Joanna and Scott are at the bottom of the stairs rushing me out the front door. Pushing is a better description. Later, I find out why. My sister got a glimpse of the living area and knew my updo would come completely undone if I saw what she saw.

We are heading toward the church and Travis sends up an SOS. Seems the boys parked where we said "Don't" and three cars were blocking Travis in our driveway. We had to circle back, take pictures of the cars and Joanna had to collect the keys from the culprits when we got to the church and send one of them back downtown to spring Travis. Meantime, Travis makes himself busy at the house.

The next day:
Travis: *Isabel, I thought I was prepared, but your living/kitchen/ dining area looked like downtown Beirut.*
He tells me it took him two hours to haul out the bottles, wipe down surfaces, stack the dishwasher, and sort the clothes as best he could. "*Even your windows were sticky.*" The entire time, I am blissfully unaware, sitting in the front pew watching David and his best friends, sober as judges on the altar of St. Rita's.

This tells you a lot about Travis.

I desperately don't want him to know how much I need him, because if that cat got out of the bag, I wouldn't be able to afford him. He knows more about what makes me tick than my sister, Gabby, or my ex. Combined. The time is quickly approaching when we might just have to get married. His insight is 100% reliable.

Anyway, I go in to see him. I am drifting again. Feeling like what was meant to be would be, no matter how hard I tried to stop it, and what wasn't meant to be wouldn't be, no matter how hard I tried to make it happen. I was powerless.

Me: *I want bangs.*
Travis: *Okay. What is going on now?*
"Bangs" is my code word for *things-are-rapidly-falling-apart.*
He refuses to give me bangs. But he gives some nuggets to consider while my hair (and my mind) are "processing." By the time I leave the salon, I am back to myself, more whole.
Travis is a perfect example of the special people who have dropped into the "along" of my life.

In the middle of twisting like a worm on a hook, I try to keep in mind that we are all "as is." Not the way we want to be, but how we are underneath it all. This also goes for circumstances. Like aging, taxes, and gravity. Another word for this is "acceptance," which I have trouble accepting. Only Gabby knows how to do this. She accepts everyone and everything exactly as they are. It's confounding.

Similarly, my mother-in-law was a pillar of acceptance and the personification of a "non-anxious presence." An unfamiliar state for someone like me. I was complaining one day about the *"What ifs?"* of my life. I might have done things differently. Zigged instead of zagged at points along the way. She looked at me. *"You know, if you change a moment you could change a lifetime."* The more I look in the rear view mirror, the truer this statement becomes, and the less I want to change a thing. Looking backward moves me forward.

So, *is the secret to happiness low expectations?* I'm not sure. What I do know is that what's real is always worth it, regardless of what we were *expecting*. The unvarnished, true, unfiltered, pure everyday stuff that we try to transcend until we come to the end of ourselves and discover we are exactly where we are supposed to be. And that often in our lives, we don't realize the significance of a relationship or situation until much later, when the experience has passed. So, I pay attention. The scrapbook is far from complete. Plenty of pages left to fill. An ongoing pursuit to find the extraordinary in both the ordinary and the *unexpected*.

In the meantime, I've learned there's more carbonation in life if you embrace your funny bone, wishbone, and backbone. Humor is both a love language and armor, dreams are fuel, and we are stronger and braver than we think.
And God is nearer than we know.